A Primer in

The Politics of
Criminal Justice

Nancy E. Marion

The University of Akron

◆

Criminal Justice Press
Monsey, New York, U.S.A.

Printed in the United States of America. No part of this
book may be reproduced in any manner whatsoever
without written permission, except for brief quotations
embodied in critical articles and reviews. For
information, contact Criminal Justice Press, Willow Tree
Press Inc., P.O. Box 249, Monsey, NY 10952 U.S.A.

Library of Congress CIP:

Marion, Nancy E.
    A Primer in the Politics of Criminal Justice/ Nancy E. Marion

        p. cm.
    Includes bibliographical references and index.
    ISBN 0-911577-32-7

  1. Criminal justice, Administration of – United States – History – 20th
century. 2. United States – Politics and government – 20th century I.
Title.
HV9950.M28 1995
364.24—dc20

                                   95-11415
                                       CIP

contents

1. Introduction 1

2. Congress and Crime 14

3. Presidents and Crime 28

4. Courts and Criminal Justice 48

5. Bureaucracies 62

6. Interest Groups 76

7. Campaigns, Elections, and the Issue of Crime 93

8. The Media and Public Opinion 106

9. Conclusion 118

    Bibliography 121

*Dedicated to Jacob Anthony: may you always have
health, happiness and love.*

One

Introduction

IN AN ELABORATE White House ceremony on September 13, 1994, President Bill Clinton signed a $30 billion "more-cops-for-America" crime bill, fulfilling one of his campaign promises. After a six year battle between Republicans and Democrats, Congress on the previous August 18 passed and sent to Clinton the bill that authorized thousands of new prison cells, established new crime prevention programs, banned assault-style weapons, extended the death penalty to 50 additional crimes, and authorized the hiring of 100,000 new police officers to fight crime (Masci 1994a; 1994b). It took no time for critics to insist that the new bill would have no effect upon the amount of violence on city streets, and that the legislation was merely a symbolic gesture to increase politicians' popularity in the months before the upcoming mid-term elections. In these elections, Democrats, who controlled the presidency and Congress, could now claim that they could no longer be labelled as "soft on crime". However, the Republicans were prepared to counter by saying that the bill was insignificant and probably ineffective in the fight against violent criminal behavior.

The politicians were not the only actors in the creation of this crime bill. The media played an active role in defining the issues, and in reporting the actions of the politicians to the public. The public not only made demands on legislators to "do something" about crime, but many also joined interest groups to further their concerns. Many interest groups were involved in the legislative process, all of which attempted to influence the final bill to represent their interests. Members of the bureaucracies were concerned, since they will be the agencies responsible for carrying out the mandates found in the legislation. Because of this, they provided testimony and expertise in the hearings surrounding the proposed bill. And although the members of the courts were not active in lobbying one side or the other, they may see the effects of the bill in terms of caseload, types of cases appearing in front of the court, or on appeals, and were therefore also interested.

The new anti-crime bill is only one example of the complexities involved in the combination between criminal justice and political science. The study of the relationships between the fields allows for an analysis of governmental outputs (policies) about crime and crime control, and is a relatively new perspective to scholars in both fields. It is relevant to scholars in both areas because each area affects the other: politicians define criminal justice and the law, and criminal events and ideas affect the behavior of politicians. The relationship, however, is much more complex than this. A greater understanding of the relationship must begin with a definition of "criminal justice" and "political science".

Criminal Justice

The study of criminal justice revolves around the knowledge of criminal behavior. Scholars in this field ask why people commit crime and what society can do to prevent further criminal behavior. It can be traced to the work of Cesare Beccaria, an Italian philosopher who was the first to make the argument that the punishment should fit the crime. He successfully argued against the use of torture, stating that the state should use the minimum amount of punishment necessary to control crime (Beccaria 1979; 1963). The American system of criminal justice is based on this idea. If someone commits a relatively minor offense (a traffic violation), that person is given a relatively minor punishment (a fine). But if that same person commits a more serious offense (a premeditated homicide), then the potential punishment is more severe (possibly death).

With the help a federal grant program called the Law Enforcement Assistance Administration (LEAA) in the 1960s and 1970s, the study of criminal justice evolved and broadened. The grant program provided money for research into criminal behavior and sanctioning alternatives to deal with criminals. Although the program ended in 1982, it provided over $8 billion to state and local law enforcement agencies to conduct research in the area and to experiment with new approaches to controlling crime ("LEAA Goes Out of Business" 1982). Because of this, criminal justice has become much broader in scope. It is now an interdisciplinary field, and draws upon knowledge from psychology, sociology, economics, anthropology, law, public policy, and political science (Misner 1981).

Political Science

Political Science is a much more developed field of study, and has been defined by Herbert Lasswell as "Who gets what, how and why" (Lasswell 1936). This means that someone or some group determines who gets what benefit, how they get that benefit, and for what reason. This also implies that a person or group has control over others. This becomes especially important in criminal justice. When defining a new crime or the potential punishment for conviction of that (or any) offense, the legislature (state or federal) has control over the citizens. They define who will be considered a criminal, what the potential minimum and maximum punishments will be (or how much freedom will be taken away), and why.

Traditional political scientists focus solely on the three major institutions of government: the president, Congress, and the courts. They describe the functions of each branch of government and how they work together to get things done. A different approach to political science examines the outputs of government, or the policies that are created by the government. This new approach examines how the three major institutions influence policy and why. For criminologists, they can use this new approach to understand the political and social forces behind criminal justice policy decisions. Why was crime put on an agenda, why was crime an issue, or what response did the government have to a particular problem? Criminologists may also want to look at the impact of those policies to determine what future policies to enact that will achieve the desired goals in the most efficient manner.

A key element in the analysis of political behavior is the concept of power. In politics, power is the ability to have a say, or to have influence, in what the government's policies are going to be (Lowi and Ginsberg 1990, 12). Each of the governmental agencies involved in the new crime bill utilized their power to influence the final bill. The president had the power to suggest elements of the bill, or to either sign it into law or veto it. The president also used his power to persuade members of Congress to vote on it. Congress had the power to alter or amend the law, and to pass it or not. The courts have the right to review the law, or elements of it, as they come to court. Obviously this is a great amount of power. But what is the source of this power as it relates to criminal justice?

Early political theorists such as Hobbes (1983), Locke (1980), and Rousseau (1964, 1983) identify a society without government which they termed a "state of nature" (Barker 1980). Locke argued that in a state of nature, life is a state of continual fear and sense of danger, where all persons are out for themselves. All persons have to spend their energy protecting themselves and their belongings from others and seeking revenge on those who have harmed them. These theorists argue that citizens enter into a "social contract" with a government, whereby they agree to surrender their right to use violence or seek revenge on others who have harmed them or their property. In return, the government promises to provide protection, peace, law and order. The government exists to enforce the social order, which means enforcing laws, punishing criminals, and defending the community. Government becomes necessary to protect people's lives. Further, Hobbes argued that the sole purpose of government is to provide an environment where citizens can pursue their natural rights, including the rights to life, to liberty, and to enjoy personal property. According to Hobbes, a government must therefore exist to provide safety for the citizens. Hobbes also wrote that when criminal acts are committed, the state must punish the offender. However, what is the best way to do this? John Stuart Mill answered this question in 1859 in his essay entitled *On Liberty*. He believed that government should use power over its citizens only to prevent harm to others. Beccaria also argued for equitable punishments that are based on the harm done by the act, as described earlier (Mill 1984, 1983).

The purpose of the law or of government, then, is to protect the citizens and their property. The writers of our Constitution (especially Franklin, Jefferson, Madison, Morris, and Hamilton) were all very educated men (Mead 1987). They were educated in philosophers such as Locke, Hobbes and Rousseau, and had many debates over the content of the Constitution (Beard 1957; 1990). They often quoted these philosophers in their debates but were most heavily influenced by the writings of John Locke on the philosophy of natural rights. The Constitution therefore defines the rights (or powers) citizens have simply because they are citizens. It also defines who can get elected and how, which will in turn influence policies created by the government. It also defines the method for creating a law that will defend the social order and the social contract. When a law is made, its purpose is to protect order.

In essence, a criminal act is a behavior that is in violation of the social contract: "(c)rime involves breaking the social contract designed to make human relations reasonably predictable and nonthreatening" (Fairchild and Webb 1985, 8). The government has power over citizens to protect the social order. Therefore, the power of the government to become involved in criminal justice stems from the Constitution.

The power of the government to be involved in criminal justice is found in the Constitution in another perspective. The document describes the powers of the branches of government, called enumerated powers. In Article I, Section 8, the document outlines the specific powers of Congress, including the powers to tax, to borrow money, and to regulate commerce. The Constitution also has implied powers, which are those powers that are necessary to perform in order to carry out the enumerated powers. For example, in order for the government to carry out the power to tax and borrow money, it must be able to incorporate (or have) a bank. Although the incorporation of a bank is not specifically listed in the Constitution as an enumerated power of Congress, it is still a constitutional act as an implied power.

There are also exclusive powers and concurrent powers found within the Constitution. An exclusive power is one which is held only by the national government, such as declaring war. No other government (i.e. state government) can declare war. Concurrent powers, on the other hand, are those powers that are held concurrently between the federal and state governments. An example of this is taxes: both levels of government can levy taxes.

The Constitution does not list "crime control" as the responsibility of the federal government, so it is not an enumerated power of Congress. But the Constitution does state that the federal government is created to "establish Justice, [and] insure domestic tranquility." In order to provide that to the citizens, the federal government must have a system to punish wrongdoers and deter future potential criminal activity. This becomes an implied power of the government.

Article I, Section 10 of the Constitution describes the powers (or activities) denied to the states. Because crime control is not specifically denied to states, and is not an enumerated power of the federal government, crime control became the responsibility of the state governments. Until very recently, then, crime control was a matter that came under the jurisdiction of the individual states, who might have sought assistance (either financial or technical) from the federal government. But there was a general understanding that state governments would handle crime issues as they deemed necessary or appropriate. This indicates that crime control was primarily an exclusive power given to the states. However, in reality, crime control was a concurrent power held jointly by both levels of government.

The federal government allowed the states to have the primary policy-making discretion in crime control until the 1960s. Since then, the federal government has used its powers more frequently and the role of the federal government in controlling criminal behavior has expanded significantly. One reason for the change in the federal response was the realization that organized crime was a powerful force in America. On November 14, 1951, there was a meeting of major crime bosses in a small upstate New York community called Appalachin ("Select Committee" 1959, 739; "Select Labor Committee" 1960, 699). It was broken up by local law enforcement officers, and twenty men were arrested. Because they had agreed not to disclose the purpose of the meeting, the men were eventually convicted of conspiring to obstruct justice and were sentenced to jail terms. The meeting and arrests made headlines across the country, proving the existence of an underworld crime organization.

Another reason for the growth of federal government's role in crime control was that Congress was holding hearings on the existence and extent of organized crime in American society. From 1957-1959, the Senate Select Committee on Improper Activities in the Labor or Management Field was created and headed by Senator John L. McClellan (D-Arkansas). Robert Kennedy acted as legal counsel to the committee. It was here that he realized the scope of the problem, and later, as attorney general, Robert Kennedy pushed for legislation to control or even eliminate organized crime. Since organized crime activities took place in many states at one time, Kennedy argued that individual states were not capable of stopping this behavior on their own. Additionally, criminal behavior that takes place across many state boundaries falls under the jurisdiction of the federal government, which furthered his argument for federal involvement ("Congress Enacts" 1961, 381).

A third reason for the increase in the federal government's role was that there was a dramatic increase in drug abuse during the 1960s, especially by white middle class America. Again, members of the federal government argued that since drug use, sales, and trafficking do not respect state boundaries, the involvement of the federal government was needed. As a result, drug control became a federal issue. There was also the recognition of the need for assistance from other countries in eliminating the drug trade. This fell under the jurisdiction of the federal government.

Not only was drug use increasing, reported crime was also

increasing during the 1960s (Scheingold 1984, xi; Wise 1991). The FBI's *Uniform Crime Report* indicated that crime rates were dramatically increasing, from 1.8 million in 1960 to almost 5 million in 1969 (Marion 1994, 9). The public's fear of crime responded. Obviously, states needed assistance to control this behavior, and they turned to the federal government for assistance.

Fourth, crime control became a central issue in many national campaigns (Cronin et al. 1981, x; Scheingold 1984, 77; Wilson 1975, 71-86). In 1964, Republican senator and presidential nominee Barry Goldwater and Democratic President Lyndon Johnson were the first to debate the crime issue at length and elevate crime control from a state concern to a national concern. Goldwater blamed the increase in crime on the Democratic administration, whom he blamed as being "soft on crime." He claimed that the Republicans, if elected, would successfully reduce crime through strict punishments and law and order programs.

In an election debate during the 1988 campaign between George Bush and Michael Dukakis, Dukakis was asked if he would support the use of the death penalty if his wife Kitty was raped and murdered. He said no, and went on a tangent about drug programs. In addition to this, Dukakis advocated prison furlough programs. An inmate on a furlough, Willie Horton, escaped from a Massachusetts prison and raped a Maryland woman and assaulted her husband. Dukakis also advocated gun control programs. Bush and his advisors used these ideas against Dukakis, and convinced the American voter that if elected, Dukakis would be soft on criminals, and crime would only continue to rise in the United States, as would each citizen's chance of becoming a victim. This was all despite the fact that Bush had led the Reagan administration's ineffective efforts to stop or control the international drug trade (especially with Noriega). Crime control has been an issue in most presidential campaigns, even as recently as the 1992 presidential campaign between Bill Clinton and George Bush.

On an academic level, scholars also recognized that political science and criminal justice are not separate fields (Cronin et al. 1981, 12). Political scientists realized that many criminal justice personnel use political means to obtain their positions, and that politics influences the justice system (Cole 1988b, 51). "A basic contribution of political science to the paradigm is the assumption that politics is an underlying factor in the criminal justice system. Like all legal and public institutions, criminal justice is "political"; it is engaged in the formulation and administration of public policies wherein choices must be made among such competing values as the rights of defendants, protection of persons and property, justice, and freedom" (Cole 1988b, 53).

"Today, increasingly, we rely on our national government to solve our society's big problems" (Cronin et al. 1981, 1). However, there is no consensus as to how the problem of crime should be solved. Disagreements as to the amount of crime and the best way to deal with that behavior continue to exist between members of the two major political parties (Cole 1988a, 1).

Liberal vs. Conservative approaches to crime control

Most candidates' approaches to crime control can be categorized as either conservative or liberal. The different approaches are an important distinction, as what they believe about crime control will determine what is found in the content of the policies (Calder 1982; Miller 1973).

Most often, the conservative approach to crime control can be attributed to Republicans (although there are Democrats who could be labelled conservative as well). They believe that the underlying cause of crime is the offender, who chooses to commit a crime through a rational decision-making process. The way to stop crime, according to conservative ideology, is through catching more criminals, convicting more of them, and sentencing them to harsh penalties. Putting "bad" people behind bars will make society safe again for the "good" people (Rosch 1985, 22; Walker 1994, 17-19; Scheingold 1984, 9-11). "(C)rime is caused by inadequate 'controls' that we have a great deal of crime because we have insufficient curbs on the appetites or impulses that naturally impel individuals towards criminal activity" (Stenson and Cowell 1991, 34).

The liberal approach, most often attributed to Democrats, emphasizes treatment or rehabilitation of offenders. The underlying causes of crime lie not with the offender, but with society, which must change in order to reduce criminal activity. Unequal social and economic conditions found in society, such as unemployment and discrimination, cause crime. Improved social conditions such as more jobs, a better economy, more access to education, and a more equal distribution of wealth is needed, as is a more equitable and humane justice system that provides due process and civil rights to all people (Rosch 1985, 21; Walker 1994, 19-20; Scheingold 1984; Dolbeare and Medcalf 1993, 52; Allen 1981).

Together

Political science and criminal justice are related in many obvious ways. First, crime is an issue discussed by state and federal governments. It is a policy area that politicians must address to appease voters. As crime continues to increase, voters demand action from politicians. They demand policies that will reduce crime in their neighborhoods. It becomes an issue more at the state and local levels because this is where most criminal policy is made. But our federal government is becoming more and more involved in the process as it becomes obvious that states cannot solve the problems without federal assistance.

Many times crime issues are essentially local issues, but they get national attention during these elections. This shows the importance of crime to the American public and thus the importance of crime in politics.

Crime and political science are also related because the criminal justice system is created by the government. The officials whom voters elect to serve them on the local, state, and national levels, pass policies that create and affect criminal justice. These policies define the agencies, the personnel, and their actions. The policies also define what behaviors are legal and what are illegal, as well as punishment for conviction of those acts defined as illegal. In effect, therefore, the government creates the system of justice in our country.

Criminal justice and political science are related because many politicians commit crimes, as was seen in the Watergate scandal, the Iran-Contra scandal, and the Abscam Scandal. Some politicians also become victims, especially of assassinations or assassination attempts. Examples of these include, of course, President Lincoln and President Reagan.

Finally, the law affects the behavior of the political actors. Law, or the outputs of government, is the ultimate goal of most political activities. People use the political arena to change or maintain a law, influence the implementation of that law, or influence how the courts interpret that law (Jacob 1986, 6).

This Book

Both the criminal justice system and the political system involve actions of the president, Congress, and the courts, as well as the bureaucracies, interest groups, campaigns and elections, and the media (with public opinion) (Jacob 1986, 7). Through their actions, elected officials are defining criminal justice. The policies they pass define what criminal justice personnel will do and how they will do it. Their actions involve the three branches of government (the executive branch or the president, the legislative branch or Congress, and the judicial branch or the courts), interest groups, public opinion, the media, and bureaucracies.

The remainder of this text will present an analysis of the major elements of American government and how they relate to criminal justice. The next chapters will focus on the three branches of government as set up in the Constitution. Chapter Two will discuss the influence of the legislative branch (Congress) on federal criminal justice policies, examining the specific laws or policies that have been created by our elected legislators to combat crime. The behavior of presidents with regard to crime control is discussed in Chapter Three. Each President since John Kennedy has had a different approach to crime, but each has addressed it to some extent. Chapter Four provides an examination of the judicial branch of government, or the federal court system.

The remaining chapters will provide an analysis of the "secondary branches" of government and how they influence criminal justice. These include the bureaucracies, interest groups, campaigns and elections, and the media (with a section on public opinion).

Bibliography

Allen, F.A. 1981. *The Decline of the Rehabilitative Ideal.* New Haven, Conn: Yale University Press.

Barker, E. 1980. *Social Contract*. New York: Oxford University Press.

Beard, C.A. and M.B. Vagts. 1957. *The Economic Basis of Politics and Related Writings by Charles A. Beard*. New York: Vintage Books, Inc.

Beard, C.A. 1990. "Framing the Constitution." In P. Woll (Ed.), *American Government: Readings and Cases*, Glenview, Illinois: Scott Foresman and Company.

Beccaria, C. 1963. *On Crimes and Punishment*. H. Paolucci (Ed.), New York: Bobbs-Merrill Co., Inc.

Beccaria, C. 1979. "On Crimes and Punishment." In J.E. Jacoby (Ed.), *Classics of Criminology*. Prospect Heights, Illinois: Waveland Press, Inc.

Calder, J.D. 1982. "Presidents and Crime Control: Kennedy, Johnson and Nixon and the Influences of Ideology." *Presidential Studies Quarterly* 12: 574-589.

Cole, G.F. 1988a. *Criminal Justice: Law and Politics*. Pacific Grove, CA: Brooks/Cole Publishing Company.

Cole, G.F. 1988b. "The Paradigm Change in Criminal Justice: The Contribution of Political Science." *Journal of Contemporary Criminal Justice* 4: 49-56.

"Congress Enacts Five Anti-Crime Bills." 1961. *Congressional Quarterly Almanac*. 17: 381-85.

Cronin, T.E., T.Z. Cronin, and M.E. Milakovich. 1981. *U.S. v. Crime in the Streets*. Bloomington: Indiana University Press.

Dolbeare, K.M. and L.J. Medcalf. 1993. *American Ideologies Today*. New York: McGraw-Hill.

Fairchild, E. and V.A. Webb. 1985. *The Politics of Crime and Criminal Justice*. Beverly Hills: Sage Publications.

Hobbes, T. 1983. *Leviathan*. C.B. Macpherson (Ed.). New York: Penguin Books.

Jacob, H. 1986. *Law and Politics in the United States*. Boston: Little, Brown and Company.

Lasswell, H. 1936. *Politics: Who Gets What, When, How*. New York: McGraw Hill.

"LEAA Goes out of Business" 1982. *Congressional Quarterly Almanac*. 38: 378-79.

Locke, J. 1980. *Second Treatise of Government*. C.B. Macpherson, (Ed.). Indianapolis: Hackett Publishing Company.

Lowi, T.J. and B. Ginsberg. 1990. *American Government: Freedom and Power*. New York: W.W. Norton and Company.

Marion, N.E. 1994. *A History of Federal Crime Control Initiatives, 1960-1993*. Westport, Conn: Praeger Publishers.

Masci, D. 1994a. "The Modified Crime Bill." *Congressional Quarterly*

Weekly Report 52: 2490.

Masci, D. 1994b. "$30 Billion Anti-Crime Bill Heads to Clinton's Desk." *Congressional Quarterly Weekly Report* 52: 2488-93.

Mead, W.B. 1987. *The United States Constitution: Personalities, Principles and Issues*. Columbia, S.C.: University of South Carolina Press.

Mill, J.S. 1984. *On Liberty*. Gertrude Himmelfarb (Ed.). New York: Penguin Books.

Mill, J.S. 1983. *Three Essays*. Richard Wollheim (Ed.). New York: Oxford University Press.

Miller, W.B. 1973. "Ideology and Criminal Justice Policy: Some Current Issues." *Journal of Criminal Law and Criminology* 64: 141-162.

Misner, G.E. 1981. *Criminal Justice Studies: Their Transdisciplinary Nature*. St. Louis: C.V. Mosby Company.

Rosch, J. 1985. "Crime as an Issue in American Politics." In E. Fairchild and V.A. Webb (Eds.). *The Politics of Crime and Criminal Justice*. Beverly Hills: Sage Publications.

Rousseau, J. 1964. *The First and Second Discourses*. R.D. Masters (Ed.). New York: St. Martin's Press.

Rousseau, J. 1983. *On the Social Contract*. D.A. Cress (Ed.). Indianapolis: Hackett Publishing Company.

Scheingold, S.A. 1984. *The Politics of Law and Order*. New York: Longman Inc.

"Select Committee on Labor Investigations." 1959. *Congressional Quarterly Almanac* 15: 731-741.

"Select Labor Committee Issues Final Report." 1960. *Congressional Quarterly Almanac* 16: 699-705.

Stenson, K. and D. Cowell. 1991. *The Politics of Crime Control*. London: Sage Publications.

Walker, S. 1994. *Sense and Nonsense about Crime and Drugs*. Belmont, California: Wadsworth Publishing Co.

Wilson, J.Q. 1975. *Thinking About Crime*. New York: Vintage Books.

Wise, C.R. 1991. *The Dynamics of Legislation*. San Francisco: Jossey-Bass Publishers.

Congress and Crime

THE LEGISLATIVE branch of government, or Congress, is defined in Article I of the U.S. Constitution and has the primary responsibility under Section 1 to create legislation. As described in Chapter One, Congress has the power to create laws that are necessary for maintaining domestic tranquility and upholding the social contract. Congress therefore can create new laws or crimes with the purpose of decreasing criminal behavior or preventing future (potential) criminal behavior. In defining new crimes, the legislative branch must also define potential punishments for that crime. In addition, they must pass laws involving criminal procedures, including rules and regulations concerning arrests, search warrants, bail, trial court proceedings, and sentencing.

Because of these important roles, the legislative branch of government is often perceived as playing a more important role in the criminal justice system than the judicial branch or executive branch. But this is not necessarily true. All three branches of

14

government must work together to influence the operation of the justice system. For example, when the legislature passes a criminal statute establishing a one year mandatory sentence for persons convicted of possession of a handgun, both the judicial and executive branches share in the implementation of the statute and its effect on the criminal justice system. The law may have been proposed by the legislative branch, but it is subject to executive approval and judicial review. Also, the sentencing involves all three branches: criminal sanctions are created by legislators, imposed and reviewed by the judiciary, and carried out by the executive branch (the bureaucratic agencies).

In addition to the power to make laws, Congress also has other powers that affect the criminal justice system. First, Congress has the power to create criminal justice agencies. The legislature establishes and controls the authority and discretion of certain administrative organizations, such as the Department of Corrections, the U.S. Parole Board, the Department of Justice, the CIA or FBI, or the U.S. Marshal's Service. Members of Congress can also vote to abolish, consolidate, or reorganize bureaucracies as they see necessary.

Congress has the ability to provide financial support for crime control programs (Steel and Steger 1988, 104). The availability of funds for such programs is always a concern. By allocating extra funds, Congress is sending a message about the importance of that program. Or, by allocating less money, Congress is showing skepticism towards a program. A good example of this is the LEAA program. It was funded by Congress during the seventies which demonstrated a commitment to expanding our knowledge about criminal behavior. But the LEAA program came under increasing criticism during the early to mid 1980s, at which point Congress refused to fund it ("LEAA Goes out of Business" 1982, 378).

Congress has the power to act as a public forum for the debate about the criminal system in the U.S. While debating a proposed bill, legislators are also debating the goal of the system: should we treat (rehabilitate) offenders or punish them? Their public debates act to inform citizens about the system, or about different aspects of the criminal justice system. The debates in Congress can also sway public opinion to support (or oppose) an idea.

Congress has power over the executive branch as it acts as a check on the behavior of the president. Congress has the ability to override a presidential veto, and can accept or deny a nomination made by the president. Individual congress members can choose to support the initiatives from the executive office, but they can also choose to support an opposing policy (Van Horn et al. 1992, 129). The members of Congress are often more influenced by the concerns of their constituents (Van Horn et al. 1992, 126; Erikson and Wright 1985, 103). Because they are re-elected every two or six years, they are, in essence, held accountable to the voters.

Some scholars have argued that the power of Congress is becoming more dispersed. The influence of the party leaders has diminished and the responsibilities of the subcommittees has increased (Koenig 1985, 51). This disperses the power to non-elected officials who work "behind the scenes" to get things done.

How a Bill Becomes a Law

The legislative process is a complex and detailed process (Redman 1973; Davidson and Oleszek 1985; Martin 1994). It begins with the formation of a proposed bill, or the "drafting" of a bill. This can be done by anyone who has an interest in suggesting a piece of legislation, including the president, a member of Congress, a private citizen, an interest group, or a bureaucratic agency. New bills are often the result of some event that identifies a loophole or new problem that must be addressed by the government. The new proposal must be introduced into the House or Senate by a friendly representative, where it is given a number for identification. Bills in the House and Senate are given sequential numbers, which are preceded by an "S" designation in the Senate and an HR designation in the House. The proposed legislation is called either a "bill" or a "resolution". Bills are more general and may be either "public bills" which affect the general public, or "private bills" which affect individuals or groups. The bill is referred to the committee that has jurisdiction over that area of legislation.

Upon receipt of the proposal, the committee chairperson refers the bill to the relevant subcommittee. The subcommittee members can hold hearings on it to allow interested parties to comment, including officials from the executive branch, members of Congress, members of interest groups, experts in a particular area, or individual citizens. The subcommittee then "marks up" a proposed bill and rewrites any components as they see necessary, or even add amendments. They will often do this in an attempt to maximize support for the bill. The members of the subcommittee must then vote on the revised version of the proposed bill. A positive vote means the bill will go on to the next step, but a negative vote means the bill "dies" and goes no further, unless reintroduced.

If the subcommittee passes the bill, it will then go back to the full committee. The members of the full committee can also "mark up" the bill, adding or deleting elements as they see as necessary. The full committee must then vote on their revised proposed legislation. As in the subcommittee, a negative vote means the bill goes no further, but a positive vote means continuing on in the process. Most bills die in committee without going any further.

For a bill to go any further in the House of Representatives, the Rules Committee must "grant a rule" for the bill. This is a set of specifications for debate and adding amendments. The Speaker of the House and the majority leader then schedule it for debate. In the Senate, scheduling for debate on the bill in the entire body is done by the majority Leader, in consultation with the minority leaders and possibly with the White House.

The members of either body then debate the elements of the bill. Some proposals are not at all controversial, and debate is limited. Other proposals have hours and hours of debate. Debate sometimes results in additional amendments added to the bill, which must each be voted upon and either accepted or rejected by the members of the House or Senate. When debate is concluded, each body then votes on the proposal. A simple majority is needed to approve it.

Since both houses must pass any proposal before it can be sent to the president, a bill passed by one house is then sent to the other house for its consideration. The other house can either accept the bill as passed by the first house or refer it to the same procedures outlined above before voting. If each house produces a different version of the bill, a "conference committee" must meet. Members of the conference committee are appointed by the leadership, and usually includes representatives of the committees that originally passed the bill plus other interested members from each house. The conference committee attempts to iron out differences in the two versions of the bill and propose a "conference version" of the bill.

Once the conference committee agrees on a compromise version, each house must accept or decline the compromise version by voting on it. If passed by both the House and the Senate, the bill is "enrolled", or published in final form on parchment by the government printing office, signed by the Speaker of the House, the vice president, or by the presiding officer of the Senate, and sent to the White House for the president's consideration.

The president has a number of options at this point. He may sign it, at which point the bill becomes law. Or the president can veto it, and return it to Congress with a message giving his reasons for the veto. If the president does not sign a bill within ten days (excluding Sundays), it becomes law automatically. However, if during that ten day period Congress adjourns, it is then considered a "pocket veto", and the bill does not become law.

If vetoed by the president, a bill dies, unless it is repassed by a two-thirds majority of both the House and the Senate. If this happens, the president's veto is overridden, and the bill becomes law without the president's signature.

All bills must complete the process during a two year congressional session. At the completion of each session, any bills that were not passed are dropped, and the next congressional session starts with a clean slate. A bill must be reintroduced if it is going to be considered again during the next session.

Once a bill becomes a law, it is implemented by the bureaucracies that have developed over time to carry out the laws created by Congress. Sometimes an individual or agency affected by the law will oppose the new policies. They have the right to challenge the law in a federal court, which then must decide upon the constitutionality of the law. Its ruling may sometimes be appealed to the Supreme Court for a final ruling.

An informal "coalition building" often takes place behind the scenes in Congress when legislation is proposed. "When legislators want to make policy, they must deal, bargain, and compromise in order to develop the several majorities required to enact legislation" (Van Horn et al. 1992, 130). Compromises must take place. "To get a bill through, committee chairs, legislative leaders, and the president (must) satisfy the parochial demands of dozens of legislators and interest groups" (Van Horn et al. 1992, 130).

The committee and subcommittee system may sound complicated and confusing, but it allows for a bill to be developed very efficiently. "Committees are powerful vehicles for policy deliberation and action. In fact, a legislature's ability to shape public policy is vastly expanded by the division of labor and development of expertise made possible by the committee and subcommittee system" (Van Horn et al. 1992, 131). The subcommittees can promote innovative policies that may not have been developed in a full floor debate (Van Horn et al. 1992, 132). The committee and subcommittee system in Congress allows the representatives to get more work done more efficiently (Price 1985; Deering and Smith 1985; Ripley 1983; Davidson and Oleszek 1985).

Brady Bill

The legislative process has been used frequently to create anti-crime bills. One example is the "Brady Bill." The event that preceded the proposal of a waiting period for the purchase of a handgun was the attempted assassination of President Ronald Reagan in March, 1981. Many versions of the bill were proposed in 1988, 1990, and 1991 (see Table 1), but the bill that was finally passed was introduced into the House in 1993 during the 103rd Congress. When introduced, the bill had 100 co-sponsors. It was given the designation HR1025, and referred to the House Judiciary Committee, and then to the House Crime Subcommittee. The subcommittee heard testimony from groups like the Bradys, who supported the bill, and the NRA, who opposed the bill. The subcommittee approved the bill on October 29, 1993, at which point it was referred back to the Justice Committee. The members of the full committee approved the Brady bill on November 4, and referred the proposed bill to the House Rules Committee where rule was granted on November 9, 1993. After only limited debate and the addition of some amendments, the House passed their version of the Brady Bill on November 10, 1993 by a vote of 238-189.

The Senate version of the Brady Bill, with 28 co-sponsors, was introduced on February 24, 1993 and given the designation S414. The Senate's version of the bill was placed on the calendar for debate on March 3, 1993, and after limited debate, the members voted to indefinitely postpone their version and pass the House version (H1025) instead (on November 20, 1993). However, the Senate added different amendments to the proposed bill than did the House. So on November 20, 1993, the Senate requested a conference, and the House members agreed on the 22nd. The conference report was filed that same day, and the House membership agreed to the new version that day. On the 24th, the Senate agreed, with the stipulation that a proposal from Senator Dole (R-Kansas) be considered at a later date. The proposal included a phasing out of the waiting period after four years. The final bill was sent to the White House and signed by the president on November 30, 1993.

The law was given the designation PL 103-159, meaning it was passed during the 103rd Congress and was the 159th bill signed during that time. The Brady Bill became effective on February 28, 1994, and was given the formal title of the Brady Handgun Violence Protection Act. As a result of the Act, the law now provides for a five day waiting period for the purchase of a handgun, which will provide for a "cooling off" period for those persons attempting to buy a gun in a period of anger. It will also allow for a background check on the purchaser to help identify those persons who should not own a gun. The law also creates a national computerized system for background checks.

Theories of Law Formation

Many theories exist that attempt to explain changes in our laws over time or the formation of new laws. Some of these ideas originate in the study of politics, whereas others find their origins in criminal justice. A brief review of these theories will provide the reader with a better understanding of the process of policy-making.

The first of these is the consensus theory. According to this theory, the majority of society's members generally agree as to what is acceptable and unacceptable behavior. The law simply crystalizes these values of acceptable behavior and forms the basis of the criminal justice system. The creation of the law is a rational process whereby the law reflects common conscious and interests of society. Therefore, the law reflects the common interest and exists for the common good. Most people, then, do not commit crimes because they believe in the laws and the system. Even without the threat of punishment, most people would not commit major crimes (Durkheim 1960; Friedman 1959).

TABLE 1
Gun Control Proposals

- HR1025 S414: Brady Bill: 5 day waiting period to have background check; also creates national computerized system.

- HR277: 7 day waiting period; no computerized check system

- S639; HR 1472: ban 9 assault weapons for 3 years

- S653: Ban over 20 assault weapons

- HR544: Multiple Handgun Transfer Prohibition Act: could only buy one gun/month

- S496:Gun taxes: increase the annual gun dealers' tax from $10 to $750

- HR737: Strict liability for Safer Streets Act: allow victims to sue manufacturers and importers in federal court

- S179: Real Cost of Ammunition Act: new tax on bullets

A second and opposing theory of law formation is the theory of conflict. This theory describes a system that includes different interests in society that come into conflict with one another. For some reason, one group is able to dominate the others. The groups work for special interests, not for the good of all members of society. In this sense the criminal law is the result of special interests who use the process to maintain their positions of power as a way to express their interests and dominate over the others. According to conflict theory, people obey laws only because they are forced to. People do not agree with the criminal statutes and laws, but comply with them because of the threat of punishment (Quinney 1969).

Three types of "powers" exist that gives one group the ability to dominate others. First is political power. This is the ability to influence the political process so that laws reflect particular interests. From this perspective, the law is imposed from the people at the top of the process. The second type of power is economic power, which is power based on economic standing. Laws are created to favor those with economic power. The third type of power is based on some special interest; for example, those who want to create laws based on religion.

A third theory of law formation is political culture. The political culture has been defined as "a set of public values about the way that politics should be conducted and the things that government should produce" (Shafer 1989). This has to do with the attitudes and beliefs of citizens about how political institutions should function, about the citizens' roles in the political process, and about the proper rules of the political game. In other words, political culture involves the beliefs, values and norms about the relationship between citizens and government. For example, some people believe that there are certain things a government ought to provide to the citizens, such as health care. Not all countries and citizens feel this way (Almond and Verba 1970; 1963).

In criminal justice, the American political culture with regard to crime control has become more conservative. This means that Americans are supporting more policies that stress law and order, strict punishment, less rehabilitation and treatment of offenders. Most citizens support policies that confirm these ideas.

A fourth theory of law formation, pluralism, finds its roots in political science. James Madison noted in *Federalist 10* that in a free society, factions (or interests) would form and, if left unchecked, could control the government. In response to this concern, a government was created that allowed for these groups to compete with one another for the ability to influence the formation of public policy (Berry 1984). This is the essential nature of pluralism: that many groups form and vie for political power and control. Our system of government is set up with multiple access points, and groups compete with one another for control of these access points and then public policy. No one group or set of groups is ever completely successful at dominating the system, so the result is policy that is a rough approximation of the public interest (Truman 1951; Dahl 1956, 1961; McKenna and Feingold 1991; Greeley 1991).

However, when too many groups become involved in the process, the government becomes divided and nothing gets done. This is the idea behind the fifth theory, called hyperpluralism. This theory states that too many groups compete for power and this actually hinders the government from being effective. Many groups, not just a few elite ones, are so strong that they divide the government and its authority. Politicians try to placate every group. Eventually they only produce confusing, contradictory, and muddled policy, if they manage to make policy at all. So the public interest is rarely translated into public policy.

Elitism, a sixth theory, is much like conflict theory, and also has a basis in political science. This was described by C. Wright Mills in *The Power Elite* (1956) and Domhoff, *The Power Elite and the State* (1990). This theory points to the fact that our society is divided along class lines. An upper class elite has power that goes beyond the formal rules of policymaking and allows members to make policy to benefit their economic class. Their power therefore finds its basis in wealth. They dominate policy decisions because they can afford to finance election campaigns and control key institutions such as large corporations. Some wealthy citizens go even further and become legislators. Criminal justice policies reflect their positions at the expense of the lower classes (Dye 1991; Bachrach 1967; Ferguson and Rogers 1986).

The seventh and final theory of law formation concerns symbolic policies. These are policies that appear to provide tangible benefits to some group(s), but actually do not (Marion 1994; Stolz 1992; Galliher and Cross 1982). They convey action on the part of legislators toward the problem at hand, when in actuality, nothing concrete is accomplished (Stolz 1983; Edelman 1985). Symbolic policies exist on two levels. First, legislation can be proposed but not passed. Legislators often propose laws that please their constituents, which allows them to respond to constituents' concerns by saying that they sponsored a bill related to that particular concern. However, sponsoring a bill "commits them to none of the difficult, time-consuming, and largely invisible activities needed to get legislation over the hurdles of subcommittee, committee, and floor passage in each house" (Nelson 1984, 19). For example, "(h)earings are held, bills are introduced, speeches are delivered, but no legislation passes" (Van Horn et al. 1992, 138).

Laws that are passed can also be symbolic. These laws fail to provide any real changes when actually implemented. Legislators pass these bills as a way to reassure constituents, or even interest groups, that their concerns are being met without legislating any real change. Politicians use symbolic policies to reassure and persuade the public (Elder and Cobb 1983). They are a way to tell the public what they want to hear, like the message that a complex problem like crime can be solved very easily and quickly (Scheingold 1984).

In the final analysis, no one theory of law formation can explain each law that is proposed or passed. It could be the case that the theory that best describes law formation changes over time. For example, the creation of the original laws may have been based on a consensus of the people. But one could point to certain time periods when conflict was at the core of the process. It could also be that the most appropriate theory depends on the crime category. *Mala in se* crimes (those that are bad in and of themselves, such as murder) are formed by consensus, but *mala prohibitae* crimes (those that are made bad, such as prostitution) are formed by conflict. Or it could be the case that there is conflict and consensus in all laws. For example, there could be consensus as to the law but conflict over the punishment.

Conclusion

Congress has many powers that can and are used to influence the criminal justice process. The primary responsibility is through its legislative powers, to create crimes such as the Brady Bill and potential punishments for conviction of those crimes. Congress has used its legislative power to a great extent to influence the justice system on both the federal and state levels. Many theories exist that attempt to explain changes in or the development of these laws made by Congress, but no single theory exists to explain its behavior in this regard.

Congress also holds secondary powers that influence the justice system, such as the ability to create or to fund criminal justice agencies. On a more theoretical level, Congress can act as a public forum for debates concerning criminal justice policies, goals, and policy alternatives.

It is obvious that Congress, as a political institution, strongly influences criminal justice policies. A complete understanding of criminal justice policies, whether they be local, state, or national, requires an analysis of congressional behavior.

Bibliography

Almond, G.A. and S. Verba. 1970. "Political Participation and Democratic Stability." In E.A. Nordlinger (Ed), *Politics and Society*. Englewood Cliffs, New Jersey: Prentice-Hall, Inc.

Almond, G.A. and S. Verba. 1963. *The Civic Culture: Political Attitudes and Democracy in Five Nations*. Englewood Cliffs, New Jersey: Prentice-Hall, Inc.

Bachrach, P. 1967. *The Theory of Democratic Elitism*. Boston, Little, Brown and Company.

Berry, J. 1984. *The Interest Group Society*. Boston: Little, Brown and Company.

Dahl, R.A. 1961. *Who Governs?* New Haven: Yale University Press.

Dahl, R.A. 1956. *A Preface to Democratic Theory*. Chicago: University of Chicago Press.

Davidson, R.H. and W.J. Oleszek. 1985. *Congress and Its Members*. Washington, D.C.: CQ Press.

Deering, C.J. and S.S. Smith. 1985. "Subcommittees in Congress." In L.C. Dodd and B.I. Oppenheimer (Eds.), *Congress Reconsidered*. Washington, D.C.: CQ Press.

Dumhoff, W. 1990. *The Power Elite and the State: How Policy is Made in America*. New York: Aldine de Gruyter.

Durkheim, E. 1960. *The Division of Labor in Society*. G. Simpson, (Trans.). Glencoe, Ill: Free Press.

Dye, T.R. 1991. "Elitism in a Democracy." In G. McKenna and S. Feingold (Eds.), *Taking Sides*. Guilford, Conn: Dushkin Publishing Group.

Edelman, M. 1985. *The Symbolic Uses of Politics*. Urbana: University of Illinois Press.

Elder, C.D. and R.W. Cobb. 1983. *Political Use of Symbols*. New York: Longman Press.

Erikson, R.S. and G.C. Wright. 1985. "Voters, Candidates, and Issues in Congressional Elections." In L.C. Dodd and B.I. Oppenheimer (Eds.), *Congress Reconsidered*. Washington, D.C.: CQ Press.

Ferguson, T. and J. Rogers. 1986. *Right Turn: The Decline of the Democrats and the Future of American Politics*. New York: Hill and Wang.

Friedman, W. 1959. *Law in a Changing Society*. Berkeley: University of California Press.

Galliher, J.F. and J.R. Cross. 1982. "Symbolic Severity in the Land of Easy Virtue: Nevada's High Marihuana Penalty." *Social Problems* 29: 380-386.

Greeley, A.M. 1991. "Building Coalitions." In G. McKenna and S. Feingold (Eds.), *Taking Sides*. Guilford, Conn: Dushkin Publishing Group.

Koenig, L.W. 1985. "Reconsidering the American Presidency and its Relation to Congress and the Bureaucracy." In P. Schorr (Ed.), *Critical Cornerstones of Public Administration*. Boston, Mass: Oelgeschlager, Gunn and Hain, Publishers, Inc.

"LEAA Goes Out of Business." 1982. *Congressional Quarterly Almanac* 38: 378-379.

Marion, N.E. 1994. *A History of Federal Crime Control Initiatives, 1960-1993*. Westport, Conn: Praeger Press.

Martin, J.M. 1994. *Lessons from the Hill: The Legislative Journey of an Education Program*. New York: St. Martin's Press.

McKenna, G. and S. Feingold, (Eds.). 1991. *Taking Sides* (Guilford, Conn: Dushkin Publishing Group).

Mills, C. W. 1956. *The Power Elite*. New York: Oxford University Press.

Nelson, M. 1984. "Evaluating the Presidency." In M. Nelson (Ed.), *The Presidency and the Political System*. Washington, D.C.: CQ Press.

Price, D.E. 1985. "Congressional Committees in the Policy Process." In L.C. Dodd and B.I. Oppenheimer (Eds.), *Congress Reconsidered*. Washington, D.C.: CQ Press.

Quinney, R. 1969. *Crime and Justice in Society*. Boston: Little, Brown and Company.

Redman, E. 1973. *The Dance of Legislation*. New York: Simon and Schuster.

Ripley, R. 1983. *Congress: Process and Policy*. New York: W. W. Norton and Company.

Scheingold, S.A. 1984. *The Politics of Law and Order*. New York:

Longman Inc.

Shafer, B.E. 1989. "'Exceptionalism' in American Politics." *P.S.: Political Science and Politics* 22: 588-594.

Steel, B.S. and M.A.E. Steger. 1988. "Crime: Due Process Liberalism Versus Law-And-Order Conservatism." In R. Tatalovich and B.W. Daynes (Eds.), *Social Regulatory Policy*. Boulder: Westview Press.

Stolz, B.A. 1983. "Congress and Capital Punishment." *Law and Policy Quarterly* 5: 157-180.

Stolz, B.A. 1992. "Congress and the War on Drugs: An Exercise in Symbolic Politics." *Journal of Crime and Justice* 15: 119-135.

Truman, D. 1951. *The Governmental Process*. New York: Knopf.

Van Horn, C.E., D.C. Baumer, and W.T. Gormley, Jr. 1992. *Politics and Public Policy*. Washington, D.C.: CQ Press.

Three

Presidents and Crime

ARTICLE II, SECTION 2 of the Constitution outlines the powers of the president. They include, for example, acting as commander in chief of the army and navy, granting reprieves and pardons, making treaties, and nominating and appointing ambassadors and other representatives of the U.S. The president's powers are not limited only to those described in the Constitution, however. The president currently has vast powers that have never been specifically defined (Cooke 1984, 64). Presidential powers have grown tremendously since the administration of Franklin Delano Roosevelt (Cronin 1990). At this point, the "Chief executives are the most visible, and in many ways the most important, actors in American Government" (Van Horn et al. 1992, 155). Although presidents are not often thought of as being influential with regard to criminal justice policy, their potential powers can have great effect upon the criminal justice system.

Probably the most important presidential power in crime control policy is the power to set an agenda about crime. This is simply a "list of things to do", or a list of issues the president would like to address in the upcoming year or term of office. "The President's agenda is a remarkable list. It is rarely written down. It constantly shifts and evolves" (Light 1983, 1). Presidents have a lot of discretion over the issues that are placed on the agenda (Light 1984; Smith 1988). Although other branches of government can influence the issues that are placed on the agenda, the presidents "dominate the agenda-setting process in the United States" (Van Horn et al. 1992, 156).

Section III, Article 2 of the Constitution requires that the president address Congress and present the programs or policies that he would like to address in the upcoming year. The "State of the Union" address is traditionally presented early in the year, after Congress convenes, and is an opportunity for the president to discuss his future agenda plans, or those things he wants to accomplish each year. The president can also address Congress periodically to appeal for the passage of legislation. Both of these types of speeches can be used to identify presidential agendas (Light 1983, 159).

Cobb and Elder (1982) distinguish two types of agendas. First is the systemic agenda, which consists of all issues that are within the power of governmental authority and that are recognized as needing legislative attention. These agendas are very vague and are simply lists of potential issues that the government could act upon. There are no alternatives or possible solutions suggested. For example, gun control is always on the systemic agenda of presidents. It is always a potential area of action for any administrations. This does not mean any action will be taken on this issue. It means only that it is an area that falls under the jurisdiction of the federal government and it is recognized as an area that needs some public attention.

The second type of agenda recognized by Cobb and Elder is the institutional or governmental agenda. This agenda is more specific than the systemic agenda and lists not only the issues of concern, but also specific alternative solutions to solve a problem. The institutional agenda is the list of concerns that will merit direct and immediate attention by the government and is a commitment for action (Eyestone 1978). Gun control often moves from the systemic agenda to the institutional after a successful assassination or assassination attempt of a president. For example, the Brady bill, which was a policy alternative to solve one aspect of the handgun problem, was suggested after the assassination attempt of President Reagan.

The president will often choose agenda issues he thinks the public wants the government to address (Van Horn et al. 1992, 160). This may apply more to those presidents who will be seeking a second term in office. But second term presidents are also worried about their legacy. Presidents are somewhat limited in creating an agenda about crime control because the primary responsibility for crime control is traditionally a states' rights issue. "Decisions made in Washington command the attention of many state and local officials because intergovernmental grants-in-aid represent about 11 percent of state and local revenue" (Van Horn et al. 1992, 160).

The president can act as a leader of public opinion, and as a moral spokesman for the public. Often the president can sense what the nation wants and be supportive of that position. By doing so, he can influence public opinion (Rossiter 1990; Page and Shapiro 1993). He must also have the public's support for success (Light 1983, 28).

Another power of the executive is to appoint loyal personnel such as cabinet and subcabinet personnel. The president nominates a variety of personnel, including the head of the FBI and CIA, which must be approved by the Senate through a confirmation process. He also nominates federal judges, including Supreme Court justices. The office of attorney general is a powerful position that has great influence over the entire Justice Department, and is also nominated by the president and approved by the Senate. By delegating authority to bureaucracies, the president can "make" policy by influencing the direction of the behavior of agencies (Van Horn et al. 1992, 10).

In addition to appointing personnel, the president can also fire or ask for the resignation from appointees that are not acting in accordance with his policy initiatives. Oftentimes, the power to fire someone is just as important as the ability to appoint. However, the president only has the power to appoint and/or fire the top officials. Most bureaucrats are civil servants with job security and are not under the direct supervision of the president.

A third power of the president to influence criminal justice policy is to grant pardons to people previously convicted of crimes. According to Article II, Section 2 of the Constitution, the president, with the help of the attorney general, can grant a pardon, commutation, remission of fine or a reprieve. President Gerald Ford used this power to grant Richard Nixon an unconditional pardon in 1974 for his involvement in Watergate, and President Jimmy Carter pardoned all Vietnam draft dodgers (Edwards and Wayne 1985). President Eisenhower commuted a death sentence to an individual with the condition that that individual never be paroled. President Nixon also granted executive clemency to James Hoffa with the stipulation that he refrain from any further union activities (Edwards and Wayne 1985).

The president also has the power to play an important leadership role in criminal justice matters. He can persuade legislators to vote for a policy, or to vote against a proposed bill (Rossiter 1990). Of course, party politics can often play a role in these activities. When Congress is controlled by a political party that is different from that of the president, this task can become all the more difficult. Presidents must rely on their power of persuasion, and they must "wheedle and cajole, relying on good ideas, political pressure, personal charm, public support, and a touch of blarney" (Van Horn et al. 1992, 9). The president relies on the party membership to get legislation through Congress (Light 1983, 27). President must work with members of Congress so representatives will not delay or reject his proposals (Koenig 1985, 51).

Finally, the president has the power to veto any criminal legislation that is sent to him from Congress. In this role he acts as a check on the behavior of the Congress. One example of this power is President Reagan's veto of an anti-crime bill (HR 3963) on January 14, 1983. He objected to a provision creating a drug czar, which was a cabinet-level office set up to oversee and coordinate all national and international federal drug enforcement activities ("Law Enforcement/Judiciary 1982"; "Law Enforcement/Judiciary 1983").

It is obvious that an executive has many potential powers to influence criminal justice policies. Some presidents have relied on these more than others. One might argue that the president's power is declining in the post-Watergate era because there is more attention paid to the president by Congress and the media. There is also more public distrust of the presidency (Light 1983, 213-4). But in terms of crime control, the presidents have used these powers to various degrees when dealing with the problems of crime. Below is a description of the presidential use of powers to influence crime control policies.

Prior to Kennedy

The federal government's role in crime control prior to the Kennedy administration was limited because crime was considered to be an issue under the authority of the individual states. Kennedy, however, was not the first president to be concerned with criminal behavior. Prior to his administration the federal government was involved with law enforcement, legislation, and research.

Federal law enforcement activity surrounded the development of agencies such as the FBI and the U.S. Marshal's Service. The FBI was originally established in 1908 by the attorney general to be the primary investigative arm of the United States government. It was concerned with investigating federal offenses such as treason, tax evasion, espionage, or offenses that crossed state lines. Most crimes continued to be under the jurisdiction of state and local officials. The U.S. Marshal's service is the oldest law enforcement agency in the country. Established in 1789, it has the responsibility for guarding the federal courts, apprehending federal fugitives, operating the Federal Witness Security Program, and transporting federal prisoners. Their activities, as with the FBI, surround only matters of federal law. The government also had its own prosecutors, called U.S. attorneys, scattered throughout the country. They also have their own prisons, which hold people convicted of federal offenses.

Some crime-related legislation was passed by Congress prior to the Kennedy administration. For example, in 1956 some laws were passed that provided punishments for confidence game swindles. Or in 1958, legislation was passed that limited the ability of inmates to file habeas corpus writs to appeal their conviction and sentence. In addition, limited research about crime and criminal justice was completed prior to the Kennedy administration. For example, in 1957, the Senate Select Committee on Improper Activities in the Labor or Management Field was given the task of looking into mob activities in major U.S. cities.

Thus, the federal government had limited involvement in law enforcement and criminal justice prior to the Kennedy administration, and only for a limited range of issues. But in the 1960s, national officials began to initiate more federal policy actions directed at controlling state-level crime. This marked the beginning of the federal government's active involvement with anti-crime policies.

Kennedy Administration

The Kennedy administration was the first to place crime control high on the governmental agenda (Steel and Steger 1988, 98). Although Kennedy focused more on civil rights, crime control was beginning to emerge as a federal issue (Cronin et al. 1981, 15). Kennedy's institutional agenda for crime control was limited to three areas: organized crime, juvenile crime, and legal counsel.

The concern with organized crime stemmed from Robert Kennedy's involvement in the McClellan hearings. As attorney General, Robert Kennedy proposed eight laws for increasing the strength of the federal government in the fight against organized crime. Five had been proposed earlier, but some were original proposals made by Robert Kennedy. These included bills that outlawed interstate travel or use of interstate facilities to establish, promote, deliver the proceeds of, or commit a violent crime to further illegal gambling, liquor, narcotics, or prostitution businesses; outlawed the shipment of firearms to or by any felon; made it a crime to flee interstate from prosecution; and outlawed the interstate transportation of all types of gambling machines (Marion 1994, 30).

Kennedy's concern with the issue of juvenile crime found its basis in his belief that it was important to stop criminal activity early before it was too late. To do this, he proposed training programs, employment and education programs, and the Peace

Corps as valid attempts to keep youth away from involvement in criminal behavior.

The third and final area of concern to Kennedy was the ability of all people, regardless of income, to be provided with adequate legal counsel if accused of a crime. Kennedy therefore proposed legislation to provide legal representation for indigent criminal defendants, and supported legislation that established a public defender's system at the public's expense.

These three issues were the primary focus of the Kennedy administration's concern with crime. This was an expansion of the crime activities of previous administrations and was the first time that crime was given a fairly high position on a president's systemic agenda. Members of the Kennedy administration, knowingly or not, were instrumental in defining and expanding the federal government's role in crime control (Calder 1982, 575). The attorney general, Robert Kennedy, was the major force behind this attention. He justified the new federal role by arguing that large organized crime syndicates were no longer problems that could be solved by the states, but demanded federal action.

Johnson Administration

Lyndon Johnson became president after Kennedy's assassination in 1963 and was reelected to the office in 1964. He wanted to continue the policies originally begun by Kennedy, but he also had to respond to the criticisms made of him during the 1964 election by Republicans that he was too soft on crime. Therefore, his crime control agenda served to expand the federal government's role in this area. Johnson's policies centered around the belief that crime control was primarily a state concern, but that the federal government should be involved in four primary areas: organized crime, narcotic and drug control, regulation of gun sales, and law enforcement activities in the District of Columbia ("Passage of Major Crime Bills" 1965).

Johnson's long-term approach to eliminating crime centered around his anti-poverty and education programs, termed the "Great Society" programs. He viewed crime as being a product of the economic and social problems that existed in society. If those core problems were addressed, a reduction in crime would naturally follow (Steel and Steger 1988, 99).

The first of four issues where Johnson saw the need for federal activity was organized crime. Johnson said that organized crime members were involved with such crimes as gambling, narcotics, fraud, loan sharking, and corruption of public officials. To increase convictions against mob members, Johnson suggested legislation that made it a crime to threaten witnesses willing to testify against mob members.

Illicit drug use was the second area of concern to Johnson, which was increasing during the period of Johnson's administration. He felt that there were some drug addicts who commit crime only because of their addiction and punishing those addicts would not be the most appropriate action. Those addicts would only be prevented from committing more crime if they were instead treated for their addiction. So Johnson recommended a "federal civil commitment" statute to provide an alternative means of dealing with those narcotic and marijuana users likely to respond to treatment and achieve rehabilitation. He called for limiting mandatory minimum sentences for marijuana possession and use, which, in a sense, is decriminalization of this drug. He also called for the decriminalization of LSD when he called for legislation making the possession of LSD and other dangerous drugs a misdemeanor. However, under this proposed legislation, the manufacture, sale, and distribution of LSD and other dangerous drugs would be classified as a felony. Johnson believed that controlling drug use was not only going to occur through treatment, and so he called for more federal agents to enforce the laws. He also called for assistance from other nations to limit drug importation into the U.S.

Firearms was the third area of concern for Johnson that was placed on his agenda. Because of the assassination of President Kennedy, Johnson made many legislative requests in this area. For example, he proposed amending the Federal Firearms Act to "prohibit firearms shipments in interstate commerce". He also called for the end of "the easy availability of deadly weapons to professional criminals, to delinquent youth, and to the disturbed and deranged". Johnson called for "(l)egislation providing for the registration of pistols" He proposed prohibiting certain classes of people from owning guns, including "minors, chronic alcoholics and the mentally ill, as well as felons and drug addicts". He called for legislation to prohibit over-the-counter sales of firearms to people who did not reside in the state in which the store is licensed, to sell handguns to people under the age of 21 and shotguns to people under 18 and to curb imports of surplus military firearms and other firearms not suitable for hunting. More restrictions were added, including the requirement that people obtain a license to purchase, possess or carry a pistol in public, or that they must carry firearms unloaded and properly encased.

The fourth and final area of concern to Johnson was crime in the District of Columbia. He thought the district could be used to test new programs and be used as a model or example for other cities. One improvement Johnson requested was to allow police to arrest suspects of serious offenses without a warrant. He called for an increase in the number of police officers, a reorganization of the corrections system, and special programs for preventing youth crime.

Beyond these four areas of concern, Johnson also asked for legislation in other areas. One area was juvenile justice. This was mostly an extension of policies first enacted under Kennedy. He supported programs that gave disadvantaged youth the chance to leave their environment. He suggested court reforms such as reform of the bail system.

A primary concern of Johnson was research into finding the root causes of crime. Little was known about the effectiveness of the agencies responsible for crime control, including the police, the courts, or corrections systems. Because of the lack of knowledge, Johnson was unsure about the proper governmental response to the problem. He suggested that legislation would be ineffective unless it was directed at the causes of crime. And to find those causes, research commissions were necessary. They were an attempt to provide more accurate knowledge of crime control to the states. Some of the research commissions and studies he supported were The President's Commission on Law Enforcement and Administration of Justice, The Commission on Obscenity and Pornography, The Study on Needs in Corrections,

The Study on the Judiciary, The National Commission to Abolish the Federal Death Penalty, and The National Commission on Reform of the Federal Criminal Laws.

Overall, although federal involvement was primarily directed to four areas during Johnson's administration, it was still an expansion of the federal role in crime control when compared to previous administrations.

Nixon Administration

Nixon's approach to crime control indicated a shift in positions from previous administrations. Nixon was a conservative Republican who suggested crime policies that reflected his conservative political ideology. He believed that criminal behavior is a rational choice made by the offender, and because of that, the offender should be punished rather than treated. An effective criminal justice system, according to Nixon, is one that relies less on treatment and rehabilitation of offenders and more on swift conviction and harsh punishments (Steel and Steger 1988, 100).

Nixon continued to expand the government's involvement in crime control, but attempted to transfer decision-making from the federal government to the state and local governments. He believed that state and local officials knew best how to solve state and local problems, which is where decisions should be made. He therefore attempted to increase the funds available for local and state law enforcement agencies.

Nixon's "law and order" stance is clear in some of the proposals he made. In the fight against organized crime, Nixon recommended that Congress double the expenditures for anti-organized crime activities, and proposed new legislation to help the federal government in this fight. He proposed that the fight against crime in the District of Columbia would be more effective if there were more judges and court personnel, more modern computer facilities in the courts, improvements in the corrections systems, and improvements in the police departments. He also supported better enforcement of the drug laws and a new juvenile code for the district.

Further support of Nixon's conservative ideology can be found in his proposals to fight drug abuse. To fight drug abuse in

American, Nixon proposed international cooperation as well as
more narcotics agents. Nixon supported legislation to prevent
pornographic materials from being sent in the mail (Daynes 1988,
50-51) and legislation that would strengthen the laws prohibiting
transporting explosives across state lines.

Despite Nixon's law and order stance, he was fairly liberal in
some of his anti-crime agenda issues. For example, he called for
programs designed around the rehabilitation of drug users rather
than simply punishment, and research into the short-and long-
term effects of drug use. Liberal ideology can also be found in
Nixon's proposals to reform the federal corrections system. He
offered a 13 point plan that included pooling resources to set up
specialized correctional facilities (for women or mentally disturbed offenders), to expand the half-way house program, and
research into discovering the most appropriate way to punish
convicted criminals. Nixon called on the states to implement
programs to educate the public about the dangers of drug use.
Nixon also supported the Legal Services Corporation, which
provided defense counsel for indigent accused criminals.

Finally, he attempted to reorganize the bureaucracies that
dealt with drug abuse. He called for the Special Action Office of
Drug Abuse Prevention to oversee all federal drug abuse prevention, education, treatment, rehabilitation, training and research
programs. He proposed a single, comprehensive agency within
the Department of Justice to lead the war against illicit drug
trafficking. This later became known as the Drug Enforcement
Administration.

Two of Nixon's agenda issues, organized crime and drugs,
found their origins in previous administrations. The monetary
relationship between the federal government and the states was
Nixon's idea, as was the attention paid to pornographic material.
The remaining three agenda issues, prison reform, criminal code
reform, and judicial reform, were all attempts to streamline the
system and ensure swift and sure punishment for convicted
criminals. So this list of agenda issues is not surprising and can
be viewed as both an expansion of the crime control policies
enacted in the Johnson administration, with some additions, as
well as a new approach to crime control.

Ford Administration

Ford served as Nixon's vice president and became president upon Nixon's resignation. He held this office for only a short period of time and was not able to fully develop a coherent set of crime control policies. Much of Ford's activities revolved around efforts to reassure the public that the illegal behavior of the Nixon administration did not apply to him. In crime control, he was a "continuation" of the Nixon administration. He supported a strong police and law enforcement role in criminal justice. But Ford did not support the extreme conservative crime control policies that Nixon suggested. Ford wanted to separate himself from Nixon, so he proposed his own ideas for crime control legislation.

Ford had many ideas for controlling crime. For example, he supported legislation that would revise the federal criminal code, and legislation to increase the rights of the victims of crime, including the financial compensation of victims. Ford was not in favor of the federal registration of guns, but he did support increased restrictions on Saturday night specials. Ford called on Congress to enact mandatory prison sentences for offenses committed with firearms, and for "hijackers, kidnappers, traffickers in hard drugs, and repeated Federal offenders who commit crimes of violence". Financial assistance to help the states battle crime was supported by the president when he proposed continuing the LEAA program (Steel and Steger 1988, 101). He supported efforts to rehabilitate offenders, especially youthful offenders.

In the fight against drug users and traffickers, Ford asked all federal law enforcement agencies to intensify their activities. In addition, a mandatory minimum sentence for drug traffickers was proposed, as was legislation to allow judges to deny bail for some people arrested for drug offenses. Ford also recognized the international aspects of drug trafficking and addressed other national leaders in combating the importation of drugs into the U.S. Congress heard requests for legislation that would require the forfeiture of cash or other property found in the possession of a narcotics trafficker. To relieve the overcrowding of court dockets and to reduce the delay in bringing criminal cases to trial, Ford proposed increasing the number of federal judges. Over-

crowded prisons were the topic of concern as well. However, Ford
did not want to give judges any reasons to keep convicted
criminals out of jail.

Despite his short presidency, it is obvious that Ford had many
proposals for federal crime policies. All of these issues had been
addressed in Nixon's administration or even Johnson's, so they
were not necessarily innovative ideas. Ford did not, then, create
any new approaches to crime control, but kept the issues alive and
on the public's mind throughout his administration.

Carter Administration

Crime did not play a significant role in the Carter administration as he did not place crime control high on his agenda (Cronin
et al. 1981, 122). The majority of those policies he did support
were based on a liberal ideology about crime control, which is
expected from a Democratic administration, but he also suggested a few conservative ideas as well. Carter spoke about many
issues, but provided little detail about his ideas. In other words,
he had many issues on his institutional agenda, but few on his
systemic agenda (Steel and Steger 1988, 101).

Carter supported the federal fight against organized crime,
but was never specific about what that fight should entail. He did
note that the drug problem was intertwined with the drug
problem in our country. Since the syndicate deals in drugs, the
war against drugs must include a war against organized crime as
well. Carter was also not specific about his proposals for juvenile
crime, other than to say that the federal government should
increase funding to attack youth crime. Carter's suggestions for
court reform were no more specific. It included reform of bail and
pre-trial detention procedures and other reforms to assure speedy
trials, increased efficiency, lower costs, and high levels of integrity in the courts. He also wanted to reform the federal criminal
code.

Carter's suggestions for handguns were more specific. He
promised federal efforts to control the manufacture, assembly,
distribution and possession of handguns. He supported mandatory sentencing for persons convicted of committing a felony with a
gun, and banning Saturday night specials. The federal govern-

ment's role in providing grants to states was different from Nixon's. Carter believed that LEAA was wasteful and inefficient, and called for the reorganization of the program. Carter also proposed changes in intelligence agency oversight and the D.C. crime program. Finally, Carter wanted a review of the federal prison policy and alternatives to incarceration such as supervised release, work release programs, and other community based programs.

In conclusion, the majority of Carter's policies find their basis in either Johnson's policies or other previous administrations. His focus on D.C. crime, organized crime, juveniles, drugs and gun control were all issues placed high on Johnson's agenda. This is not surprising since both Carter and Johnson were Democrats who believed in the liberal tenets of crime control. Most of the remaining issues, including LEAA, judicial reform, revision of the criminal code, reform of federal corrections, and speedy trials were all issues developed in previous administrations.

Reagan Administration

President Reagan served in office for eight years, and therefore had sufficient time to influence criminal justice policies made by the federal government. Reagan returned to many of the conservative ideals first espoused in the Nixon administration, including a focus on law enforcement and punishment rather than treatment of offenders. Reagan believed that crime was a chosen lifestyle, and that punishments had to be made more certain, swift and severe if crime was to be reduced in the nation.

Probably one of the most, if not the most, important issue on Reagan's agenda was drug use. He said we needed a reorganization of federal agencies for a comprehensive attack on drug trafficking and organized crime. As part of an omnibus anti-crime bill he proposed increased sentences for drug traffickers. The bill also included the establishment of sentencing guidelines, reform of bail policies, reform of the insanity defense, limited assistance to states, a restoration of the federal death penalty, a modification of the exclusionary rule, and reform of habeas corpus (Steel and Steger 1988, 102).

Reagan believed strongly in the Second Amendment right to

bear arms and the right of citizens to own guns. However, he also believed in strict punishments for those people who used firearms for illegal behavior. Therefore, he proposed mandatory sentences for commission of armed felonies.

He wanted legislation to deter child pornography. "In his 1984 State of the Union Message, President Reagan suggested that parents needed reassurance that their children would not be abducted or become objects of child pornography... He reassured the audience that his administration would enforce all antipornography laws" (Daynes 1988, 53). He established a commission to investigate the effects of obscenity on society.

Reagan felt that victims of crime deserved more attention from the federal government, and supported legislation to do that. And finally, Reagan supported allocating millions of dollars for prison and jail facilities so the mistake of releasing dangerous criminals because of overcrowded prisons would not be repeated.

Although Reagan's agenda may be perceived as short, when compared to other agendas, there were more crime control issues addressed during his administration than any other. He was successful in continuing to expand and broaden the federal government's role in crime control.

Bush Administration

George Bush was Reagan's vice president for eight years, and upon taking the office of president, he had an approach to crime control similar to Reagan's. Bush did not have a terribly strong agenda for crime control, but the agenda continued to be as conservative as under the Reagan administration. Bush's agenda revolved around two major issues: drugs and an omnibus anti-crime bill. Two minor agenda issues were firearms and violent crimes.

His conservative approach could be seen in his proposals to curb illicit drug use in the U.S. He supported mandatory sentences and the death penalty for major drug traffickers and doubling the mandatory penalties for the use of semi-automatic weapons in crimes involving violence or drugs. Bush also asked for drug treatment programs, urban school anti-drug programs, and education programs.

The comprehensive anti-crime bill proposed by Bush included many areas that had been separate issues in previous administrations. For example, the bill included changes in the exclusionary rule, the death penalty, habeas corpus appeals, and the insanity defense. Bush wanted to double the mandatory penalties for the use of a semi-automatic firearm during the commission of a crime, and to allow for pretrial preventive detention for cases involving firearms. He also supported mandatory sentences for the theft of a firearm.

Finally, Bush proposed adding more Alcohol, Tobacco, and Firearms Department agents, additional U.S. Marshals, and additional FBI agents to help in the fight against violent crime. Additional assistant U.S. attorneys and criminal division attorneys were sought as well.

Clinton Administration

Bill Clinton was inaugurated as president in January, 1993. At this writing, he has only had two years to act on the problem of crime control. However, during that short time he has been successful in pushing a crime bill through Congress. It is obvious from his comments about the bill and from statements made during the 1992 presidential campaign that Clinton can be labelled a "conservative liberal" with regard to crime control, as his proposals consist in liberal policies with a conservative twist. During his inaugural address, he called on young people to give "a season of service" (Zuckman 1993, 218). Apparently he was referring to a suggestion made during his campaign that the student loan program evolve into a national service trust fund. Under this program, students would repay student loans by volunteering in their communities. However, many questions were unanswered about the program: should it be a mandatory program? How large of a program would it be? Who should participate? When would students work - before or after college? (Zuckman 1993).

Early in his term, Clinton restructured the Office of National Drug Control Policy, or "drug czar" office. He elevated the office to Cabinet status, giving it more prestige. But at the same time he also cut the size of the office from 146 employees to 25 (Idelson

1993a, 320).

In the area of gun control, Clinton supported a ban on assault weapons and a waiting period for handgun purchases (Idelson 1993c, 602). He felt so strongly about it that during an economic address to Congress, Clinton detoured to support the proposed 5 day waiting period for handgun purchases, as set forth in the Brady Bill (Idelson 1993d, 1021). Originally part of the anti-crime bill proposed by Clinton, the Brady Bill was passed separately by Congress, and signed by the president on Nov. 30, 1993.

To fight crime on the streets, Clinton suggested legislation on August 11, 1993, to put 100,000 new police officers on the streets. The proposal also included more money for drug abuse prevention and treatment programs, an expansion of death penalty provisions, additional funding for more police officers, and a revision of the habeas corpus provisions (Wong 1993, 2979). Earlier, Clinton proposed cuts in the State Justice Institute (created to improve the efficiency of courts), slowing the rate of prison construction, freezing grants by the Office of Justice, and elminating some state anti-crime programs that would be dupli-cated in the new crime bill (Idelson 1993b, 378).

After months of debate by Congress, the proposed anti-crime bill was passed and sent to the president for his signature. The final bill provides for the hiring of 100,000 new police officers, additional prison construction, crime prevention programs, an assault weapons ban, a state registration of sex offenders, an expansion of the death penalty provisions, a "three strikes and you're out" provision that mandates life imprisonment for a third violent felony, and a stipulation that juveniles over the age of 12 who commit certain violent crimes be tried as adults (Masci 1994a, 2490).

The provisions of the new crime bill demonstrate that Clinton, despite being a Democrat, has taken a conservative approach to crime control. This includes stricter punishments rather than a traditional liberal approach of relying on treatment and reha-bilitiation of criminal offenders. At this point, he still has two years to complete his first term as president, and it remains to be seen what, if anything, he will propose regarding crime control. But he was successful in steering two major pieces of anti-crime legislation through Congress during the short time in office to date.

Conclusion

A major power of presidents to influence the criminal justice system is through the agenda setting responsibility. In varying degrees, all presidents since Kennedy have attempted to create legislation that would reduce crime in the U.S. It is obvious that each president had the power to affect criminal justice to a great extent. Kennedy was successful in expanding the federal response to crime, and with the help of his brother, Robert, he began to define and expand the role of the federal government in crime control. Johnson continued the policies of Kennedy, but also was effective in expanding the role of the federal government. His approach was modified by Nixon, who was labelled as our first "law and order" president. Nixon spoke of harsh punishments, but also supported liberal policies. Ford also suggested a lenient, yet still conservative, approach to crime control. Carter's policies were a mix of both liberal and conservative approaches. He did not place crime control high on his agenda, so federal crime control policy was put on hold during this administration.

Reagan again put crime control on the forefront of American public policy. He returned to the more conservative approach taken by Nixon, but he also succeeded in further expanding the federal government in the issue. Bush had only one term to define his crime control approach, but for the most part he maintained the policies supported by Reagan. Clinton was inaugurated on January 18, 1993, and has been labelled a "conservative liberal" regarding his crime control policies.

Beyond agenda setting, presidents can also influence criminal justice by appointing personnel, granting pardons, playing a leadership role, or in vetoing legislation. These powers, although less obvious than agenda setting, have potentially enormous impact on criminal justice matters when used together. From this discussion, it is easy to see that the president, as a political institution has great impact on criminal justice.

Bibliography

Calder, J.D. 1982. "Presidents and Crime Control: Kennedy, Johnson and Nixon and the Influences of Ideology." *Presidential Studies Quarterly* 12: 574-589.

Cobb, R.W. and C.D. Elder. 1982. "Issue Creation and Agenda Building." In J.E. Anderson (Ed.), *Cases in Public Policy-Making*. New York: Holt, Rinehart and Winston.

Cook, E.F. 1984. *A Detailed Analysis of the Constitution*. Totowa New Jersey: Rowman and Allanheld, Publishers.

Cronin, T.E. 1990. "The Swelling of the Presidency: Can Anyone Reverse the Tide?" In P. Woll (Ed.), *American Government: Readings and Cases*. Glenview Illinois: Scott, Foresman and Company.

Cronin, T.E., T.Z. Cronin, and M.E. Milakovich. 1981. *U.S. v. Crime in the Streets*. Bloomington: Indiana University Press.

Daynes, B.W. 1988. "Pornography: Freedom of Expression or Societal Degradation." In R. Tatalovich and B.W. Daynes (Eds.), *Social Regulatory Policy*. Boulder: Westview Press.

Edwards, G.C., III and S.J. Wayne. 1985. *Presidential Leadership*. New York: St. Martin's Press.

Eyestone, R. 1978. *From Social Issues to Public Policy*. New York: John Wiley and Sons.

Idelson, H. 1993a. "Downsizing of Drug Czar Office Draws Mixed Reviews." *Congressional Quarterly Weekly Report* 51: 320.

Idelson, H. 1993b. "Special Report: Law Enforcement." *Congressional Quarterly Weekly Report* 51: 378.

Idelson, H. 1993c. "Reno's Confirmation Was Easy: The Hard Work Lies Ahead." *Congressional Quarterly Weekly Report* 51: 601-602.

Idelson, H. 1993d. "Gun Rights and Restrictions: The Territory Reconfigured." *Congressional Quarterly Weekly Report* 51: 1021-1026.

Koenig, L.W. 1985. "Reconsidering the American Presidency and its Relation to Congress and the Bureaucracy." In P. Schorr (Ed.), *Critical Cornerstones of Public administration*. Boston, Mass: Oelgeschlager, Gunn and Hain, Publishers, Inc.

"Law Enforcement/Judiciary." 1982. *Congressional Quarterly Almanac* 38: 20-21.

"Law Enforcement/Judiciary." 1983. *Congressional Quarterly Weekly Report* 41: 149.

Light, P.C. 1984. "The Presidential Policy Stream." in M. Nelson (Ed.), *The Presidency and the Political System*. Washington, D.C.: CQ Press.

Light, P.C. 1983. *The President's Agenda*. Baltimore: The Johns Hopkins University Press.

Marion, N.E. 1994.*A History of Federal Crime Control Initiatives, 1960-1993*. Westport, Conn: Praeger.

Masci, D. 1994a. "The Midified Crime Bill." *Congressional Quarterly Weekly Report* 52: 2490.

Page, I.B. and R.Y. Shapiro. 1993. "Presidents as Opinion Leaders." In R.B. Ripley and E.E. Slotnick (Eds.),*Readings in American Government and Politics*. Belmont, CA: Wadsworth Publishing Company.

"Passage of Major Crime Bills Not Likely in 1965." 1965.*Congressional Quarterly Weekly Report* 23: 1881-1884.

Rossiter, C. 1990. "The Presidency—Focus on Leadership." In P. Woll (Ed.), *American Government: Readings and Cases*. Glenview, Illinois: Scott, Foresman and Company.

Smith, H. 1988. *The Power Game*. New York: Ballantine Books.

Steel, B.S. and M.A.E. Steger. 1988. "Crime: Due Process Liberalism Versus Law-and-Order Conservatism." In R. Tatalovich and B.W. Daynes (Eds.), *Social Regulatory Policy*. Boulder: Westview Press.

Van Horn, C.E., D.C. Baumer, and W.T. Gormley, Jr. 1992.*Politics and Public Policy*. Washington, D.C.: CQ Press.

Wong, B. 1993. "Anti-Crime Bill Chronology." *Congressional Quarterly Weekly Report* 53: 2979.

Zuckman, J. 1993. "The President's Call to Serve is Clear but Undefined." *Congressional Quarterly Weekly Report* 53: 218-221.

Four

Courts and Criminal Justice

The judicial branch of government, the courts, is defined in Article III of the U.S. Constitution. This sets up one Supreme Court and as many lower or inferior federal courts as Congress deems necessary. The courts have jurisdiction over federal laws, to all cases affecting ambassadors, maritime cases, land grant cases, and cases between the U.S. and states, and between states. In cases where ambassadors or a state is a party, the Supreme Court has original jurisdiction. These cases begin in the Supreme Court and the court has the obligation to take. The justices can also decide whether decisions from the lower courts present questions or conflicts important enough or of such constitutional nature as to warrant the court's consideration on review. This is termed appellate jurisdiction. In these situations, the court cannot look for cases to review: it must wait for cases to come to it.

In the U.S., there is a dual court system, meaning that there are two systems operating independently of each other. First, there is the state court system, which includes minor courts (sometimes referred to as misdemeanor courts), general trial level courts, intermediate appellate courts, and state supreme courts.

On the federal level, there are three levels of courts. The lowest level court is the district court, which is similar to the trial courts in the states. These courts hear only cases concerning violations of federal laws such as spying, lying to Congress (during a hearing, for example), or treason. These courts were established under the Constitution. More specialized courts such as the U.S. Claims court, which hears only cases involving monetary claims made against the U.S., are also considered to be district courts.

The second level of federal court system is that of the federal court of appeals. When a case goes to trial and the federal district court renders a judgement, the defendant may appeal the judgement in the appeals court. Most criminal procedures are established by the appellate courts. Appellate courts interpret the law and determine whether it meets constitutional requirements.

The highest level of federal courts is the U.S. Supreme Court, which is also an appellate court. There are nine justices serving on the Supreme Court, who are appointed for life terms. Presently, the justices include:

Name of Justice	Year / President Appointed	Conservative or Liberal
Rehnquist	1971 Nixon	
	1986 Reagan	C
Souter	1989 Bush	C
Breyer	1994 Clinton	L
Stevens	1975 Ford	L
O'Connor	1981 Reagan	C
Scalia	1986 Reagan	C
Kennedy	1988 Reagan	C
Thomas	1991 Bush	C
Ginsburg	1993 Clinton	L

The conservatives on the court include Rehnquist, Scalia, Kennedy, Souter, Thomas, and O'Connor, all of whom were nominated by Reagan or Bush except Rehnquist, who was originally appointed by Nixon but chosen to serve as Chief Justice by Reagan. Liberal judges include Breyer, Stevens, and Ginsburg, who were appointed by either Ford or Clinton. This means that the Court is currently dominated by conservative justices, who make decisions based on that philosophy.

The ideology of the justices serving on the Supreme Court changes over time. Under Chief Justice Earl Warren (1953-1969), the majority of justices serving on the court were liberal, so the decisions coming down from the court supported individual and minority interests. The justices were dedicated to protecting free expression (Daynes 1988, 48) and were concerned with expansion of due process and legal counsel rights of defendants (Steel and Steger 1988, 74). For example, with regard to the exclusionary rule, the court made policy that respected the rights of privacy of citizens. It "made the protection of the constitutional right to due process the basis of many of its decisions on the rights of the accused" (Steel and Steger 1988, 82). The Warren court extended the rights of the accused under the due process clause of the Fourteenth Amendment, incorporated the protections found in the Bill of Rights to the state courts, made decisions that mandated desegregation of public schools, and upheld the rights of defendants in state criminal cases. Overall, the court made far-reaching social changes.

In the election of 1968, Nixon attacked the Warren Court as too liberal (O'Brien 1993, 36). As president, Nixon appointed four people to the Court: Warren Burger, Harry Blackmun, Lewis Powell and William Rehnquist. They were chosen because they were considered to have conservative judicial philosophies (O'Brien 1993, 36).

Under Nixon, the Burger Court (1969-1986) shifted the focus to a more conservative ideology but it also served as a transitional court between the liberal Warren court and the more conservative Rehnquist court (O'Brien 1993, 121). The Burger Court was less protective of individual rights. Its decisions implied that individual rights are not absolute, and it made decisions that loosened Fourteenth Amendment due process rights (Steel and

Steger 1988, 83).

The differences between the two Courts can be seen in their decisions concerning the rights of persons taken into custody. The Warren Court decided in *Miranda v. Arizona* (1966) that prior to interrogating suspects, officers must inform suspects of their rights. The Burger Court modified Miranda, in *Harris v. New York* (1971). Now defendants who take the stand can be questioned even if they never received Miranda warnings (Steel and Steger 1988, 83). The Burger Court upheld *Miranda* in general, but gave greater flexibility to help police and prosecutors convict accused criminals.

When President Reagan appointed Justice Kennedy, he achieved a more conservative Court. This was made more certain when President Bush nominated Souter and Thomas, who also hold conservative views (O'Brien 1993, 117). Together, Bush and Reagan nominated more than half of the 761 member U.S. judicary (Brewster and Brown 1994, 226). On the whole, "(t)he appointees of Presidents Ronald Reagan and George Bush have helped to form a seemingly invincible conservative majority that has moved with increasing boldness to execute a conservative political agenda" (Biskupic 1991b, 101).

The current chief justice, William Rehnquist, has been in that position since 1986. Under Rehnquist, the Court has shifted further to the right and is becoming more conservative (Moore 1993). For example, with regard to the exclusionary rule, the Rehnquist Court decisions now allow evidence to be admitted into trial because the legal technicalities allow guilty defendants to escape conviction (Steel and Steger 1988, 74). The more conservative Court has upheld the basic rights of counsel, fair trials, and juvenile offenders, including Miranda rights, but has given greater flexibility to the police and corrections personnel, making changes in the death penalty, unreasonable searches and seizures, and the exclusionary rule. Through its decisions, the Court "basically said it was up to Congress and the states to do the policy-making. Unlike the more liberal Warren and Burger Ccourts, it declined to write law that would address social dilemmas" (Biskupic 1991b, 101).

Power

When they make a decision, whether it be conservative or liberal, judges are determining who will pay a fine and the level of that fine, who will spend time in an institution and for how long, or even who will be afforded due process rights and who will not. Since they are deciding benefits, judges are political actors with power. It is now recognized that judges have distinct power in their own sense. To a great extent, the power judges have is determined by the position they hold (i.e. what type of judge they are).

Of all the actors in the criminal justice system, judges, as a whole, have the greatest prestige. Symbols of judicial power exist in all courts. For example, the robes, high benches and demands for decorum and honorific forms of address each serve to give judges an aura of power and authority. However, judicial power extends beyond this.

Appellate judges have great amounts of power to influence citizens. More than other judges, these judges, when deciding cases, make policy that affect everyone, not just the parties involved in the case. For example, when the Supreme Court decided in *Roe v. Wade* (1973) that a woman's right to an abortion was constitutionally protected, the decision applied to all American citizens, not just those involved in that case. However, the justices do not have the power of enforcement and therefore cannot enforce their decisions. Instead, they must rely on others to do that. Therefore, their power depends largely on the public's acceptance of their decisions.

The justices on the Supreme Court have special powers. The primary power of the Supreme Court is called judicial review. This is the power of the Supreme court to declare state and federal laws invalid or unconstitutional if they conflict with the Constitution. It stems from the 1803 case of *Marbury v. Madison*. As a result of the case, all acts of Congress are subject to review by the Court (Murphy 1964).

The chief justice of the Supreme Court has specific power because of the position he holds. For example, the chief justice presides over Court conferences and is the first to speak. If the chief justice votes with the majority in a decision, then he assigns the task of writing that decision to a more junior justice (Davis 1993).

District level courts also have significant amounts of power, in many ways more than appellate judges. This is because there are many more of them and they have great discretion (Van Horn et al. 1992, 195). Most of the decisions made by the trial level courts are not appealed, meaning that their decisions are final. They also have the ability to appoint court personnel, reporters, bailiffs, clerks and sometimes probation officers. This means they have great power over the direction of the court in that manner.

Some would argue that the power of the judges is declining. They point to the substantial increases in the number of criminals in the system, which in turn creates more work for judges. Because of this, court backlogs are lengthy. Judges have found themselves in a position where they must work harder for less respect. It has also created a system whereby others involved in the case (i.e. police, prosecutors, correctional personnel) can have great amounts of discretion in deciding a punishment. This has also served to reduce the power of judges.

Others would argue that the power of judges is actually increasing. This is because judicial decisions now affect many more people than in the past, and the potential impact of these decisions is much greater. In other words, the judges have much more ability to influence policy than previously.

Decisions

Regardless of his or her position, each judge has the power to make policy. Through their decisions, the courts are making policies (Murphy 1964; Johnson and Canon 1984). Even when they decide not to hear a case, they are in essence making policy by upholding a previous decision. It is commonly assumed that the justices are making neutral decisions based upon the law and the Constitution. If this were the case, however, the law would never change or evolve. In reality, the law is based upon the preferences of the justices involved in a case (Smith 1992, 3). Most federal judges belong to the party of the president who appointed them, and they remain faithful to their party while in office. Although this loyalty may vary from issue to issue, party identification is the single best predictor of judicial voting behavior (Van Horn et al. 1992, 195).

Because they are appointed for life terms and do not have to face reelection, the courts can often make policy in areas where legislators cannot. For example, many very controversial issues such as abortion, school prayer and civil rights are frustrating for legislators. No matter which way they vote, or which side they support, many of their constituents will be angered. This means that they often cannot vote on these issues. The courts, however, are free to act in these areas. The courts do not have to take the safest political route, either.

In the case of civil rights legislation made during the 1960s, many legislators were hesitant to show support for either side of the issue. They worried about angering voters at home. The courts, however, did not have to worry about that. They were free to make social policy such as *Brown v. Board of Education* (1954) that mandated desegregation of public schools.

Although most judges would state that they do not make decisions based on party ideology, it has been demonstrated that Republican judges tend to decide cases differently than Democratic judges do. Democratic judges are more likely to decide cases with a more liberal slant. This means they are more supportive of the criminal defendants, the disadvantaged, and people who claim to have been deprived their civil liberties (Van Horn et al. 1992, 199). Democratic judges also tend to favor the defense in criminal cases (Baker and Meyer 1980, 51). Republican judges, on the other hand, are more likely to decide cases with a more conservative slant. This means they support longer sentences, fewer appeals, etc. They are also more likely to favor the prosecution (Baker and Meyer 1980, 152). Further, conservative courts prefer to have social policies defined in the state courts (Biskupic 1991a, 104). They favor the government's interest over the interests of individuals. Liberals support the reverse policy (Biskupic 1991a, 104).

Politics

It is obvious that political ideology plays an important role in the judicial decision-making process. However, it is commonly assumed that federal judges are not political actors, but rather are neutral actors who make decisions based on the law or precedent. This is not necessarily true. Judges are often involved in various forms of politics as part of their jobs. Beyond playing an important role in the decisions that are made, politics also plays a role in the judicial recruitment process, and with relationships between other actors in the political system, including Congress and the president.

Recruitment

In *Federalist 78*, Alexander Hamilton argued that judges should be appointed for life because they should not have to worry about public opinion and reelection. This would allow them to make decisions based on the law alone. Currently, federal judges are placed on the bench by an extremely political process that often involves great political conflict and competition. When a vacancy arises, the president has an extensive search for a qualified person and nominates someone to fill the position. The nomination then goes to the Senate Judiciary Committee for hearings and a vote. If the vote is positive, the nomination is referred to the entire Senate for hearings and a vote. The nominee must be confirmed by the Senate by a simple majority for confirmation.

A potential judge's legal ability is weighed against other factors such as personal and ideological compatibility with the administration, the support or opposition in Congress, and with demands for representation on the basis of geography, religion, race, gender and ethnicity (O'Brien 1993, 66). Requirements for appointment include professional qualification, personal and political friendship, representation of geographic region, religion, party affiliation, and political and ideological compatibility (Birkby 1985). "No section of the nation can be left without a justice for a long period of time, and no section should have a disproportionate number of members sitting on the same court" (Birkby 1985, 244). Most nominees have held other prominent state or federal positions prior to the appointment. But they have also made themselves known to the president (or an advisor) in some other way. For example, they may have served the administration or the president in some way, or made decisions in the past that reflected the president's ideology (Glick 1993, 135; Edwards and Wayne 1985).

Usually the nominee is of the same political party as the president. This is because the court will be making policy, and the president wants those policies to reflect his ideology. The nominee can also represent a population of the president's supporters. For example, President Johnson nominated Thurgood Marshall to the court, the first black Supreme Court justice (Glick 1993, 135).

A description of some recent Supreme Court nominees demonstrates the political nature of the process. Judge Robert Bork was nominated in 1987 by President Reagan to serve on the Court when Justice Lewis F. Powell, a moderate, resigned. Bork was a graduate of University of Chicago Law School, was a professor of law at Yale University, and served as solicitor general in the Nixon administration. The approval of Bork meant that the court would then have a majority of conservatives and would change the policies of the court for many years to come. Many groups got involved in the nomination process, including civil rights groups, women's groups, and abortion rights groups to voice support or opposition for the nomination.

During the confirmation hearings, Bork discussed how he would vote on specific cases. In so doing he contradicted his past behavior, which was conservative (O'Brien 1993, 114). Because of the contradictions, 1,925 law professors signed letters opposing Bork (O'Brien 1993, 115). The Judiciary Committee eventually voted 9 to 5 against the nomination and he was defeated in the full Senate by a vote of 58 to 42.

Reagan then nominated Judge Douglas H. Ginsburg to serve on the court. Ginsburg had many personal and professional ties to Bork, and it was expected that would be much like Bork in terms of his decisions and actions (O'Brien 1993, 116). He was a more promising candidate, but he admitted to smoking marijuana and was talked into withdrawing his nomination. Finally, Judge Anthony Kennedy was confirmed to replace the retiring Powell.

Another example of politics playing a role in judicial nominations is the nomination of Clarence Thomas to serve on the

Supreme Court. Justice Thurgood Marshall retired in 1991 from the Court, and President Bush chose Thomas, a black American and Republican, to replace Marshall. Many groups got involved in the process, including the NAACP (National Association for the Advancement of Colored People), NARAL (National Abortion Rights Action League), and NOW (National Organization of Women), which were all groups that came out against Thomas. The National Urban League and the ACLU stayed uncommitted.

During the Senate Judiciary committee's hearings, Thomas emphasized his personal success at overcoming poverty, and gave very guarded answers to the Judiciary Committee's questions (Biskupic 1991d, 18). Thomas even stated that he never seriously thought about the constitutionality of *Roe v. Wade* ruling on the right of a woman to choose an abortion (O'Brien 1993, 119; Biskupic 1991c, 98). After almost two weeks of hearings, the Senate Judiciary Committee voted 7 to 7 along party lines and decided to send the nomination to the full Senate without a recommendation.

Anita Hill, a black law professor at the University of Oklahoma, then came forward and told the Senate Judiciary Committee that Thomas had sexually harassed her when they worked together at the Department of Education and the Equal Employment Opportunity Commission in the early 1980s. The judiciary committee held additional hearings to find out more about the charges, but were unable to determine if the charges were true or not. The Senate voted to confirm Thomas with a vote of 52 to 48.

President Bush then nominated David Souter of New Hampshire to serve on the Supreme Court when Justice William Brennan, a liberal justice, retired from the court in 1990. It was thought that Bush successfully nominated a "safe" nominee with an uncontroversial background and moderate political attitudes, which made him a nominee that was more likely to be accepted by the Senate (Glick 1993, 136). Souter had been New Hampshire's attorney general and a member of the state supreme court. The Senate Judiciary Committee voted 13 to 1 to recommend him (with Senator Kennedy dissenting), and the whole Senate confirmed him by a vote of 90 to 9.

Appointment to lower federal courts is not as complex or as public. Because there are so many of them, the president and the

Senate cannot spend as much time on each individual judge as with nominees to the Supreme Court. Lower federal courts are also not seen as having such a great impact on national policy as the Supreme Court. But these appointments can become political as well. One example is Daniel Manion, who was nominated to be a judge on the Seventh Circuit Court of Appeals by President Reagan in 1986. Manion had little experience in the federal court and had no prior judicial experience. He had no record of publications in law reviews, and some of his legal briefs given to the Senate had spelling and grammatical errors. Further, he was accused of being too conservative. He suggested posting the Ten Commandments in the public schools, and was associated with the John Birch Society. A vote was taken in the Senate, and the results were a 47 to 47 tie. Senate rules allowed for a reconsideration of the vote, which was put off for several weeks. The second vote was again a tie, this time a 49 to 49 tie. This was broken by Republican Vice President Bush in Manion's favor.

Relations with Presidents and Congress

In addition to the nomination process, politics is evident in the relationships between the justices, the presidents and Congress. The political nature of the Supreme Court's relationships finds its basis in the structure of the government. The Court oversees the president and Congress; Congress and the president interact with the Court. The Congress and the president can react to decisions by the Supreme Court and thereby reshape the policies created by the court. For example, the Supreme Court, in *Texas v. Johnson* (1989), decided that burning a flag was protected under the First Amendment as a form of symbolic speech. Both the president and members of Congress reacted to the decision, and proposed a constitutional amendment to prevent flag burning. This did not pass, and a federal statute was created instead. The Supreme Court reacted to their new law, and in *United States v. Eichman* (1990), again struck down the federal statute. Congress again proposed a constitutional amendment to prohibit flag burning. In the end, Congress lacked the required number of votes to pass the amendment (Smith 1992, 131-2). This activity demonstrates the reactions each branch of government has towards the others.

The relationship between the president and the justices has special characteristics. Every president must pay particular attention to the courts because they make policy. Some of that policy-making may run counter to the president's preferences and may even invalidate those preferences, which could hurt the president's policy agenda. The presidents can use the courts to legitimize the executive and legislative policies they develop (Birkby 1985, 240). The president can use his power of appointment to influence the direction of court decisions and further his agenda (Birkby 1985, 242). Conflict betweenpthe president and courts tends to arise when a new president presents a new set of policies, but the court is still more representative of an older policy agenda (Birky 1985, 241).

A special relationship can also develop between chief justices and the presidents through an advising role. Both presidents Kennedy and Johnson went to Chief Justice Warren for advice, and Chief Justice Burger sent notes to President Nixon about judicial reform ideas (O'Brien 1993, 127). Justices also either volunteer or agree to serve as quasi-diplomats, arbitrators of foreign and domestic controversies, and heads of commissions (O'Brien 1993, 134). For example, Chief Justice Warren was the head of the commission to investigate the assassination of President Kennedy. However, public opinion is opposed to justices acting as presidential advisers or helpers (Scigliano 1984). Many people criticized the advisory role of the justices, and for the most part, this practice has stopped (Edwards and Wayne 1985).

Since both the president and the judiciary are responsible for the execution of laws, they must develop a positive working relationship. The president is an active agent in law enforcement. He has subordinates in the bureaucracies who oversee the laws. Justices, on the other hand, are passive in their involvement. They make decisions which many people watch and change their behavior accordingly. The Court also supervises the work of others, primarily lower federal courts. These courts can order writs, make sentences (Scigliano 1984), but the Court must rely on the president to enforce their decisions (Edwards and Wayne 1985; Johnson and Canon 1984).

Conclusion

It is obvious that the courts, probably more than any other political institution, have many opportunities to influence the operations of the criminal justice system. Their exact power depends on the type of judge they are, however. District judges make decisions that impact many citizens, and appellate judges can review these decisions to determine their constitutionality through the powers of judicial review. These decisions depend upon the personal ideology of the judge and on the make up of the court. In either case, the judges are making public policy that can affect many people.

Although presumed to be neutral, the behavior of judges is very political. Politics is evident in the recruitment process and in relations with both the president and Congress. It is obvious that the courts constitute a political institution that has enormous impact on the functioning of the criminal justice system.

Bibliography

Baker, R. and F.A. Meyer, Jr. 1980. *The Criminal Justice Game*. North Scituate, Mass: Duxbury Press.

Birkby, R. 1985. "The Courts: 40 More Years." In M. Nelson (Ed.), *The Elections of 1984*. Washington, D.C.: CQ Press.

Biskupic, J. 1991a. "Bush Boosts Bench Strength of Conservative Judges." *Congressional Quarterly Weekly Report* 49: 171-174.

Biskupic, J. 1991b. "1990-91 Term Marked by Surge in Conservative Activism." *Congressional Quarterly Weekly Report* 49: 1829-1831.

Biskupic, J. 1991c. "Democrats to Push Thomas on Abortion, Other Views." *Congressional Quarterly Weekly Report* 49: 1826-1828.

Biskupic, J. 1991d. "Thomas Hearings Illustrate Politics of the Process." *Congressional Quarterly Weekly Report* 49: 2688-2689.

Brewster, L.G. and M.E. Brown. 1994. *The Public Agenda*. New York: St. Martin's Press.

Davis, S. 1993. "Power on the Court: Chief Justice Rehnquist's Opinion Assignments." In R.B. Ripley and E.E. Slotnick (Eds.), *Readings in American Government and Politics*. Belmont, CA: Wadsworth Publishing Company.

Daynes, B.W. 1988. "Pornography: Freedom of Expression or Societal Degradation?" In R. Tatalovich and B.W. Daynes (Eds.), *Social Regulatory Policy*. Boulder: Westview Press.

Edwards, G.C., III, and S.J. Wayne. 1985. *Presidential Leadership*. New

York: St. Martin's Press.

Glick, H.R. 1993. *Courts, Politics and Justice.* New York: McGraw Hill, Inc.

Johnson, C.A. and B.C. Canon. 1984. *Judicial Policies: Implementation and Impact.* Washington, D.C.: CQ Press.

Murphy, W. 1964. *Elements of Judicial Strategy.* Chicago: University of Chicago Press.

O'Brien, D.M. 1993. *Storm Center.* New York: W.W. Norton and Company.

Scigliano, R. 1984. "The Presidency and the Judiciary." In M. Nelson (Ed.), *The Presidency and the Political System.* Washington, D.C.: CQ Press.

Smith, C.E. 1992. *Politics in Constitutional Law: Cases and Questions.* Chicago: Nelson-Hall Publishers.

Steel, B.S. and M.A.E. Steger. 1988. "Crime: Due Process Liberalism versus Law-and-Order Conservatism." In R. Tatalovich and B.W. Daynes (Eds.), *Social Regulatory Policy.* Boulder: Westview Press.

Van Horn, C.E., D.C. Baumer, and W.T. Gormley, Jr. 1992. *Politics and Public Policy.* Washington, D.C.: CQ Press.

Five

Bureaucracies

BUREAUCRACIES ARE often called the fourth branch of government because they possess so much power in the governmental process. The founding fathers did not create a bureaucratic system in the Constitution, but rather left this responsibility to the members of Congress (Edwards and Wayne 1985). Congress eventually decided that there should be executive departments with a single appointed official, called a secretary, who would be nominated by the president and approved by the Senate. The president would be the only person who could remove the secretary. The first agency to be created was the State Department, with nine employees in addition to the secretary (Wilson 1978, 55).

Bureaucracies have developed over time as a way to divide responsibilities among specialized groups so that tasks get done more efficiently, and so that complex problems will be more simplified (Gawthrop 1969, 8). The primary role of the bureaucracies is to implement or carry out the policies adopted by Congress. This includes "issuing and enforcing directives; disbursing funds; making loans; awarding grants; signing contracts; collecting data; disseminating information; analyzing problems; assigning and hiring personnel; creating organizational units; proposing alternatives; planning for the future; and negotiating with private citizens, businesses, interest groups, legislative committees, bureaucratic units, and even other countries" (Edwards and Wayne 1985, 349; see also Anderson 1990). But a secondary role is to influence legislation. We expect bureaucracies to be politically neutral, but in fact they function within an environment of fragmented political power. As a result, bureaucracies and bureaucrats have substantial power (Long 1978).

Weber (1947) presents classic characteristics of a theoretical bureaucracy. They include specific, fixed rules concerning functions; a hierarchy organization with superior-subordinate relationships; a formal internal management using written documents that serve as permanent records; and a high degree of administrative expertise on the part of officials concerning their responsibilities and the bureaucratic rules (Merton 1970, 59). No bureaucracy has all of these characteristics to the fullest extent, but each bureaucracy exhibits at least some of these characteristics.

Powers of Bureaucracies

There are three main functions of bureaucracies that help to determine their power. The most prominent task is to implement the laws and policies as described by the courts or legislatures. In this task, bureaucracies are simply carrying out the laws or policies enacted by the legislators (Jacob 1986, 248). However, legislators rarely consider implementation problems when creating a new law (Van Horn et al. 1992, 145). When laws are passed by Congress, they are often vague or unclear (Edwards and Wayne 1985; Reich 1994). They will pass laws that have inconsistent goals, or even goals that are operationally meaningless (Gawthrop 1985, 52). The laws rarely include the necessary steps required to put a program into effect (Gordon 1992, 49). This means that bureaucrats must interpret the statutes and then decide the specific details about those policies before they can be implemented. In doing so, they must design programs to carry out the mandates of Congress or the courts. Often, the agencies will gather public comments about a bill, then compose any revisions or details they feel are necessary (Jacob 1986, 253).

When making decisions about the programs, bureaucrats must make policy decisions. They have power based on this authority (Jacob 1986, 248; Van Horn et al. 1992, 94). Bureaucrats at the top of an agency can impose their ideas on an agency or department.

The power to create policy details is often seen in a positive light. First, the bureaucratic agencies are the people who deal with the problem(s) every day. They know the specifics of the problems and the best way to solve the problem, probably even better than legislators who tend to be more removed from the problem. Second, bureaucrats can enforce their regulations (Jacob 1986, 257). Bureaucracies can withhold benefits, permits, or financial assistance to ensure compliance with a law. Courts, however, have to rely on voluntary compliance.

However, this power is often seen in a negative light. The bureaucrats holding this power are the unelected officials. They do not have to respond to public opinion, and cannot be removed from office by the public. They do not make policy based on the wishes of the American public, but on their own ideas. Some consider this to be a form of unrepresentative government.

Another function of the bureaucracies is to settle disputes (Jacob 1986, 248). Many agencies can adjudicate disputes in quasi-judicial proceedings that are much less formal than a courtroom setting. The case is heard by one or a group of officials, usually without a lawyer or specific rules of procedure. The decision may be appealed to an appellate court, which is more formal. Usually a bureaucracy is one of the parties in the dispute, and the case is a test of administrative policy (Jacob 1986, 258-60).

The party that loses a case in an administrative hearing has little choice but to comply with the ruling. If the party does not, the agency can take further action against him and assess increased fines or other punishment. In cases where the losing party depends on the agency for a certain benefit, the agency can also withhold that benefit until the party complies with the ruling (Jacob 1986, 263-4).

The management of the agency has a profound impact on the cases heard by the administrative courts. Since they are responsible for defining the policies to be implemented by the agency, they are, in a sense, defining what issues will be brought to the court. In addition, the management is responsible for setting the agenda for the agency, and deciding what cases to pursue and which to overlook. They also decide if a case should be handled formally or informally. This is also influenced by the fact that many of the administrators are friendly with other officials. Cases involving acquaintances are often handled informally rather than formally (Jacob 1986, 264).

A third power of the bureaucrats is to draft or help to draft proposals for bills or at least assist a legislative aide in doing so. The bureaucrats are often involved with identifying problems that need to be addressed by Congress, or identifying plausible alternative solutions to solve a problem. Because of their expertise and knowledge of the problem, bureaucrats have the power to influence legislators when creating or working on ("marking up") a proposed bill (Van Horn et al. 1992, 94; Gordon 1992, 53; Rourke 1978, 79; 1984).

These three functions point to the amount of power bureaucracies have, as well as their discretion to influence public policy. It is obviously quite extensive.

Sources of Power

The power of bureaucrats stems from at least four sources. First, power can be developed from a strong clientele (Van Horn et al. 1992, 94; Gordon 1992, 55; Simon, Smithburg and Thompson 1978, 18). If a clientele is satisfied with the service provided to them, they often try to protect the bureaucracy from angry politicians or the public and in return expect favorable action from the bureaucracy. Power can also come from Congress (Gordon 1992, 54). Bureaucrats get power from Congress through the appropriations process. With a stable or increasing budget, bureaucrats can spend money for personnel and for other purposes (Simon, Smithburg and Thompson 1978, 18). They must continually lobby for support from committees, subcommittees, and individual members of Congress. They can do this by responding quickly to their requests for information, or by implementing programs efficiently.

Congress has some limited powers over the bureaucracy. For example, Congress has the power of appropriations. Through this power, Congress determines if a bureaucracy will live or die (Ripley 1983). Congress also has the power to order an audit of an agency through the General Accounting Office to determine if funds are being used in the most appropriate way, for example. In addition, Congress can hold hearings in which bureaucrats may have to answer for their actions (Davidson and Oleszek 1985). Finally, Congress also has influence in the nomination process for top bureaucratic positions. Its rejection of a nominee can be embarrassing to the administration (Ripley 1983).

Bureaucratic power can stem from the president. Since the top officials in the majority of bureaucracies are appointed by the president, the majority of bureaucrats must respond to the president. We assume that bureaucratic behavior will follow the intent of the executive. The president, therefore, can give some agencies more power by giving them more (or less) authority to act.

The president also has the power to remove personnel. For example, President Clinton accepted the resignation of Surgeon General Joycelyn Elders for a difference of opinion they had about the direction of policy (Popkin 1994). The president also has legislative power that allows him to shape legislation surrounding the bureaucracy's behaviors. He can also restructure the bureaucracy.

Presidents often view bureaucracies with distrust. They feel the bureaucracies are working for their own interests rather than those of the nation or the president. Some studies have shown that bureaucrats are opposed to the policies pursued by the presidency (Nelson 1984, 23). The president has a number of options to control the bureaucracies. First, he can appoint bureaucrats who have his values and will protect his interests. Second, he can ask members of the White House staff to monitor the activities of the bureaucracy. Third, the president can create organizational structures within the White House that will take the lead in policy areas that are of particular concern to him (Rourke 1984, 340).

Finally, bureaucrats get power from the general public. Through its vote, the public can become a source of support or opposition for ideas or proposals that are pursued by a bureaucracy (Simon, Smithburg and Thompson 1978, 20).

Weaknesses

There are some weaknesses of bureaucracies (Gulick 1985, 95-96). First, top officials in major bureaucracies often become wrapped up in their departments and become oblivious to outsiders who may offer suggestions or help. They may also become too specialized and technologically advanced that they feel too self-important and lose sight of the bureaucratic environment (Gawthrop 1969, 25). This can also trickle down to lower level employees so that the attitude is conveyed to the general public who has contact with that agency. Second, excessive reliance on rules and regulations, red tape, and paperwork each prohibit a bureaucrat from personalizing each case. Instead, there is little if any flexibility to personalize each case. People become numbers and are treated impersonally. There is also little flexibility based on different environments.

Each bureaucracy must fight with other agencies for resources from Congress. Especially in recent years, when money has been more limited, bureaucracies must constantly defend their programs as being effective and cost efficient.

Bureaucracies have been criticized for a lack of tangible goals. In the private sector, a goal is often motivated by profit. But this motivation does not exist in non-profit groups. In addition, there is often a change of administrators which will lead to a lack of continuity or stability within the agency (Gawthrop 1969, 58).

Finally, the issue of bureaucratic accountability is a concern. This refers to holding the bureaucracy responsible for what it does. The president and Congress have some control over the bureaucracy, but their influence remains limited. It often becomes difficult to oversee the extent of activities carried out by the bureaucracies.

Examples of Bureaucracies

The power of bureaucracies extends to criminal justice in many ways. Below is a brief description of some federal bureaucracies related to criminal justice. This is not a comprehensive analysis of the bureaucracies that are involved with criminal justice areas, but simply a sampling of those bureaucracies that have potentially enormous impact on the justice system.

DEPARTMENT OF JUSTICE

The Department of Justice was created in 1870 to handle all criminal prosecutions and civil lawsuits in which the U.S. had an interest. Among the sub-bureaucracies found in this department include the attorney general, the deputy attorney general, the solicitor general, the Bureau of Prisons, the FBI, the Marshals Service, and the Office of Justice Programs.

ATTORNEY GENERAL

The U.S. attorney general is the head of the U.S. Department of Justice, and therefore also a member of the president's cabinet. S/he is nominated by the president and confirmed by the Senate. The office of the attorney general was created in 1789 in the Judiciary Act, which established the federal judicial system of the U.S. and the office of attorney general. This person was to be the legal counselor for the government. In 1870 it was changed to the Justice Department, which the attorney general now heads.

Today, the attorney general is the chief law enforcement/legal officer in the nation. Although some people refer to it as the "largest law office in the world," it only has one client: the Government of the U.S. The attorney general still counsels the Congress and president and lower courts in matters of law and national policy. The office gives advice and opinions to the president and to other administration officials. In most important cases, the attorney general will appear in front of the Supreme Court. The attorney general is also concerned with the safety and security of citizens in the U.S. and abroad, and for applications of parole.

DEPUTY ATTORNEY GENERAL

The attorney general has a deputy attorney general and other staff who assist in the functions required for the office. The deputy attorney general serves as acting attorney general when needed. The functions are largely administrative duties, assisting the attorney general in the administration of the Department of Justice and coordinating the activities of the departments. Other tasks include screening applications and making recommendations for appointments to the federal judiciary, checking the backgrounds of appointees and of legal personnel, acting as a liaison with Congress, and testifying in front of Congress in proposing/ marking up proposed bills.

SOLICITOR GENERAL

The solicitor general acts as the government's lawyer. This person decides what government cases are appealed to the Supreme Court, represents the U.S. in front of the Supreme Court, supervises the creation of briefs and legal documents, decides if the U.S. should appeal in all cases it loses before the lower courts, supervises all oral arguments, and decides if the U.S. should file a brief as "amicus curiae" in any appellate court (Scigliano 1984). The solicitor general is an appointed position, and must go through the nomination/confirmation process in the Senate.

BUREAU OF PRISONS

The mission of the Bureau of Prisons is to protect society by carrying out the judgements of the federal courts through providing confinement services to committed offenders. One foremost responsibility is to provide safe, secure and humane correctional institutions for individuals sentenced to serve time in them. This includes overseeing medical programs and environmental, health, safety, and sanitation services. In addition, the Bureau also assists state and local corrections agencies by providing technical information concerning institutions, including the development of plans, programs, and policies concerning the construction and staffing of new facilities. The National Academy of Corrections, the Institute Information Center, and the National Jail Center are all programs run by the Bureau of Prisons that provide additional information about prisons. Alternatives to the traditional correctional facilities, such as community corrections programs and boot camp programs have been topics of research. Finally, the federal prison industries (UNICOR) is owned by the federal government, which provides employment and training opportunities for inmates confined in correctional facilities. In this program, the inmates are involved with the manufacture of many products, including furniture and electronics.

FEDERAL BUREAU OF INVESTIGATION

The Federal Bureau of Investigation (FBI) was formed in 1909, and is the most widely publicized law enforcement agency. It is the investigative unit of the Department of Justice, but is not a national police force. In 1934, it was given the authority to carry guns, serve subpoenas, make seizures, serve warrants, and make arrests. The FBI currently has jurisdiction over all matters in which the U.S. may be an interested party and is responsible for investigating violations of federal statutes. These include espionage, sabotage, treason, civil rights violations, murder and assault of federal officers, mail fraud, robbery and burglary of federally insured banks, kidnapping, and interstate transportation of stolen vehicles and property.

The FBI was given the authority to collect and analyze statistics on the amount of reported crime in the nation each year. The *Uniform Crime Reports* are published annually and include statistics on the number of reported crimes, arrests, law enforcement officers killed or injured, and other information. The FBI also runs a comprehensive crime laboratory that tests evidence such as hairs, fibers, blood and drugs. It collects and maintains a fingerprint file that can be used for identification purposes by local law enforcement officers. Finally, the FBI helps to train local law enforcement officers (Senna and Siegel 1990, 198-99).

U.S. MARSHALS SERVICE

The Marshals Service is the oldest federal law enforcement agency. In September, 1789, Congress passed the Judiciary Act, which provided for a federal court system. Along with supporting personnel (judges, clerks, district attorneys), each district court was also assigned a marshal. The marshal was ordered to carry out "lawful precepts" given to him. The marshals eventually acquired additional responsibilities, including custody of federal prisoners, provisions of the physical needs of the court, disbursements of court funds, and executing prisoners (Ball 1978). Today, the service is responsible for providing support and protection for the federal courts (security for judges, personnel and juries), apprehending federal fugitives, operating the Federal Witness Protection Program, maintaining the custody of and transporting federal prisoners, executing court orders and arrest warrants, seizing, managing and selling property taken by the government by drug traffickers and other criminals (the Justice Department's National Asset and Seizure and Forfeiture Program), and responding to emergency circumstances (terrorists) through the Special Operations Group (Sommer 1993).

OFFICE OF JUSTICE PROGRAMS

The Office of Justice Programs (OJP) was created by the Justice Assistance Act of 1984, and is supposed to identify evolving criminal justice issues, develop and test new alternatives to solve those problems, evaluate programs and responses, provide information to state and local governments, and to maximize efficiency and effectiveness in the criminal justice system as a whole. There are five major offices within OJP that are all interrelated and work together to improve criminal justice. These are:

a. *Bureau of Justice Assistance.* The Bureau of Justice Assistance provides financial and technical assistance to state and local governments, with a special emphasis on violent crime and serious offenders. The money can also be used to control drug abuse and trafficking.

b. *Bureau of Justice Statistics (BJS).* This bureau was created to collect, analyze and publish statistics about crime, criminal offenders, and victims. They are responsible for the *National Crime Survey*, published yearly.

c. *National Institute of Justice.* The NIJ is the primary sponsor of research on crime in the federal government. It sponsors and conducts research, evaluates policies and provides training. It has a computerized database of documents and will provide custom searches or document loans. They also have a public reading room and referral services.

d. *The Office of Juvenile Justice and Delinquency Pro-*

grams. Just as it appears, the OJJDP is the primary federal agency for addressing juvenile crime in the nation. They also work with the problem of missing children. The OJJDP was created by the Juvenile Justice and Delinquency Prevention Act of 1974.

e. *Office for Victims of Crime.* This office carries out the Victim and Witness Protection Act of 1982, and oversees the crime victims funds established to financial reimburse victims of criminal behavior. They also address the issues of improving the treatment of crime victims.

U.S. CUSTOMS

The U.S. Customs Service enforces the provisions of the Tariff Act of 1930 (Department of Treasury 1991). It's mission is to "protect the nation's revenue by assessing and collecting tariffs on goods brought into the country (and to seize) smuggled goods" (Prince and Keller 1989, 235). They are also responsible for regulating the movement of persons or merchandise between the U.S. and other countries; protecting domestic industry and workers from unfair competition from foriegn manufacturers; and protecting the American public and environment against hazardous products (Department of Treasury 1991). In the fight to keep drugs out of the country, customs agents identify and apprehend suspicious persons at ports of entry. Working with agencies such as the Drug Enforcement Administration (DEA) or Immigration and Naturalization Service (INS), customs officers identify the flow of drug dollars into the country, which has led to seizures of drugs and proceeds from drug activity (Prince and Keller 1989, 236). Customs is also involved with enforcing the laws that prohibit the importation and possession of obscene and pornographic materials, particularly those that involve children (Daynes 1988). Officers cannot determine what is pornographic, but can only check suspicious packages and work with the post office to withhold mail, or they can prohibit the importation or transportation of any obscene material into the U.S.

In 1965, the customs service initiated international involvement. At present, the agency has international activities in many countries, including Saudi Arabia, Philippines, Ethiopia, Argentina, Indonesia, Thailand, Mexico, Japan, Hungary, and many other countries. Their activities include advisory assistance programs, technical and managerial training, executive observation programs, conferences, narcotic detector dog programs, multilateral and bilateral agreements, and participation in international organizations (U.S. Customs Service 1984, 1989).

THE BUREAU OF ALCOHOL, TOBACCO AND FIREARMS (BATF)

The Bureau of Alcohol, Tobacco and Firearms (BATF) was established in 1972. Originally, jurisdiction over these areas was held in the IRS, but was transferred to this new bureaucracy. BATF helps control sales of untaxed liquor and cigarettes and has jurisdiction over the illegal sale, importation, and criminal misuse of firearms and explosives (Senna and Siegel 1990, 200). It has two sections: regulatory enforcement and criminal enforcement. The Bureau publishes a quarterly report to announce official rulings and procedures. It publishes decisions, legislation, administrative matters and other items of interest (Department of Treasury, 1992). In 1981, Reagan proposed abolishing the BATF by either transferring responsibility back to the IRS or dividing responsibilities between the U.S. Customs Service and the Secret Service. Neither proposal was passed by Congress (Spitzer 1988, 135).

Conclusion

Bureaucracies have great discretion and ability to impact criminal justice. Through their powers of implementing Congressional mandates, settling disputes, drafting legislative proposals, bureaucrats are able to create or change policies influential to the justice system. Many bureaucracies have been created by Congress to carry out their policies designed to control criminal behavior, as described above. Some of these agencies are old, but most are relatively new. All have increasing responsibilities as the needs of the nation become greater. In sum, bureaucracies are another example of a political institution that impacts criminal justice.

Bibliography

Anderson, J.E. 1990. *Public Policymaking: An Introduction*. Boston: Houghton Mifflin Company.

Ball, L.D. 1978. *The United States Marshals of New Mexico and Arizona Territories, 1846-1912*. Albuquerque: University of New Mexico Press.

Davidson, R.H. and W.J. Oleszek. 1985. *Congress and its Members*. Washington, D.C.: CQ Press.

Daynes, B.W. "Pornography: Freedom of Expression or Societal Degradation?" In R. Tatalovich and B. W. Daynes (Eds.), *Social Regulatory Policy*. Boulder: Westview Press.

Department of Treasury. 1991. "United States Customs Service: Mission and Organization." Washington, D.C.: Department of The Treasury, U.S. Customs Service.

Department of Treasury. 1992. "BATF Quarterly Bulletin." Washington, D.C.: U.S. Department of Treasury.

Edwards, G.C, III, and S.J. Wayne. 1985. *Presidential Leadership*. New York: St. Martin's Press.

Gawthrop, L.C. 1969. *Bureaucratic Behavior in the Executive Branch*. New York: The Free Press.

Gordon, G.J. 1992. *Public Administration in America*. New York: St. Martin's Press.

Gulick, L. 1985. "Policy Roles of Public Administrators." In P. Schorr (Ed.), *Critical Cornerstones of Public Administration*. Boston, Mass: Oelgeschlager, Gunn and Hain, Publishers, Inc.

Jacob, H. 1986. *Law and Politics in the United States*. Boston: Little, Brown and Company.

Long, N. 1978. "Power and Administration." in F.E. Rourke (Ed.), *Bureaucratic Power in National Politics*. Boston: Little, Brown and Company.

Merton, R.K. 1970. "Bureaucratic Structure and Bureaucratic Behavior." In E.A. Nordlinger (Ed.), *Politics and Society*. Washington, D.C.: CQ Press.

Nelson, M. 1984. "Evaluating the Presidency." in M. Nelson (Ed.), *The Presidency and the Political System*. Washington, D.C.: CQ Press.

Popkin, J. 1994. "A Case of Too Much Candor." *U.S. News and World Report* 117: 31.

Prince, C.E. and M. Keller. 1989. *The U.S. Customs Service: A Bicentennial History*. Washington, D.C.: Department of the Treasury; U.S. Customs Service.

Reich, R.B. 1994. "Policy Making in a Democracy." In F.S. Lane (Ed.), *Current Issues in Public Administration*. New York: St. Martin's

Press.

Ripley, R.B. 1983. *Congress: Process and Policy.* New York: W.W. Norton and Company.

Rourke, F.E. 1984. "The Presidency and the Bureaucracy: Strategic Alternatives." in M. Nelson (Ed.), *The Presidency and the Political System.* Washington, D.C.: CQ Press.

Rourke, F.E. 1978. *Bureaucratic Power in National Politics.* Boston: Little, Brown and Company.

Scigliano, R. 1984. "The Presidency and the Judiciary." In M. Nelson (Ed.), *The Presidency and the Political System.* Washington, D.C.: CQ Press.

Senna, J.J. and L.J. Siegel. 1990. *Introduction to Criminal Justice.* St. Paul: West Publishing.

Simon, H.A., D.W. Smithburg, and V.A. Thompson. 1978. "The Struggle for Organizational Survival." In F.E. Rourke (Ed.), *Bureaucratic Power in National Politics.* Boston: Little, Brown and Company.

Sommer, R.L. 1993. *A History of the U.S. Marshals.* Philadelphia: Courage Books.

Spitzer, R.J. 1988. "Gun Control: Constitutional Mandate or Myth?" In Tatalovich, R. and B.W. Daynes (Eds.), *Social Regulatory Policy.* Boulder: Westview Press.

U.S. Customs Service. 1989. "International Accomplishments, 1982-1989." Washington, D.C.: U.S. Customs Service.

U.S. Customs Service. 1984. "The International Activities of the U.S. Customs Service." Washington, D.C.: U.S. Customs Service.

Van Horn, C.E., D.C. Baumer, and W.T. Gormley, Jr. 1992. *Politics and Public Policy.* Washington, D.C.: CQ Press.

Wilson, J.Q. 1978. "The Rise of the Bureaucratic State." In F.E. Rourke (Ed.), *Bureaucratic Power in National Politics.* Boston: Little, Brown and Company.

Interest Groups

THE FRAMERS OF the Constitution, particularly James Madison, were concerned about creating a government which had the potential of being controlled by a few individuals. Madison, in *Federalist 10*, wrote about the dangers of factions, or groups of citizens who were able to monopolize the legislative process. He argued that in a developing society, it is inevitable that social classes will form, and that these social classes would form factions to protect their interests. These factions, it was argued, could be controlled by allowing all the groups the opportunity for involvement in the decision-making process. The groups would then balance each other out, resulting in policy that would be in the common good (Berry 1984; Hamilton et al. 1961).

Today, the factions described by Madison are referred to as interest groups, and can be defined as groups of individuals or citizens with a common interest or goal, that seek to influence public policy in some way (Berry 1984). These groups work with legislators to develop policies that are beneficial to both. They may wish to influence legislation because of professional concerns, economic gain (i.e. manufacturers of anticrime equipment), or for moral commitment (Steel and Steger 1988, 92). They do not seek to influence all policies, but only those that will affect their particular interests.

Three theories exist that attempt to explain the influence of interest groups in the legislative process (see Chapter One). The first of these is pluralism, which holds that American government has many access points for interest groups to affect the legislative process. Public policy is the result of the struggle between groups that each vie for their own concerns. The resulting policy reflects citizen's concerns. Hyperpluralism refers to the state of chaos that occurs when too many interest groups have too many access points to the process and they bring the system to a standstill. When this occurs, the policy that results is not reflective of citizens' interest, but rather a mish-mash of bits and pieces of different ideas. Finally, elitism is the theory that holds that public policy decisions are made by a small group of individuals, i.e. wealthy citizens, that act in their own self-interests rather than in the interests of all people. These people have the ability to influence legislators to such an extent that the resulting policy decisions are made to benefit a select few.

Interest groups attempt to affect policies through a variety of methods (Key 1990; Schlozman and Tierney 1993; Davidson and Oleszek 1985). An interest group may publicize an issue in the mass media and make appeals for public support for or against a policy. The group may make mass mailings to members and non-members to provide information on potential legislation, and urge action. The group may ask their membership to send letters, telegrams or postcards indicating support (or lack thereof) of a particular bill. They can make the public and legislators aware of an issue and demand action (Hallett and Palumbo 1993, xvi). With all of these activities, the groups are attempting to motivate the public to support their cause, called grassroots lobbying (Eagleton 1991; Wittenberg and Wittenberg 1990). This can be very effective since legislators receive opinions from all types of constituents rather than just members of one interest group.

Groups may also become involved in various election activities. One election activity that interest groups use to influence legislation donating money to the campaigns of candidates who support their cause (Ripley 1983). For example, in 1990 the NRA spent $18,000 to fight the reelection bid of Peter Smith (R-Vermont) after he supported a bill proposing an assault-weapons ban (Biskupic 1991, 183). They also contributed $36,108 on Tom Tauke in his campaign against Tom Harkin for Iowa senator; $23,380 for Jesse Helms over Harvey B. Gantt in N. Carolina; $19,742 for Rudy Boschwitz over Paul Wellstone in Minnesota; and $15,686 for Bill Schuette over Carl Levin in Michigan. On the whole, in 1990 the NRA spent $916,135 on campaigns (Biskupic 1991, 183).

One opposing interest group, Handgun Control Inc., contributed $178,882 on campaigns that same year (Biskupic 1991, 183). They spent $18,587 against Jolene Unsoeld (D-Washington) who supported a bill to weaken a ban on semiautomatic weapons (Biskupic 1991, 183). In the other races noted above, Handgun Control spent $9,000 on Paul Simon, $6,000 on Levin; $5,000 on Gantt; and $5,000 on Harkin (Biskupic 1991, 183).

The most important activity interest groups use to influence legislation is lobbying. Lobbying consists in attempts to influence policy in the executive and legislative branches of government. Sometimes many groups will combine forces and create a temporary coalition that attempts to achieve an objective (Eagleton 1991).

Interest groups can get directly involved in the legislative process through testifying at a subcommittee or committee hearing, or even during full House or Senate debate in very controversial bills. They can either help to draft a bill, or can draft a bill on their own. They can talk to members of Congress either formally or informally and attempt to persuade them on how to vote. This may involve submitting written recommendations with supporting documentation. A study of the proposal to reform the criminal code indicates that 218 individuals and interest groups gave testimony on at least one of the proposals (7 proposals were included in this study). Most groups appeared only once or twice. But twelve groups testified three or more times (Melone and Slagter 1983).

Interest groups play an important role in policymaking. Some have great influence in the final legislation that is passed, whereas others have relatively little. The amount of influence they have revolves around a number of factors, one of which is money. Simply put, groups with more money have potentially more power. They can hire more lobbyists, hire more staff members, or purchase more ads in the public media. Groups can also give "money" to candidates by providing campaign work and volunteers to help in the campaign. Information is another factor that can affect the amount of influence a group has. Information can help a group member lobby a legislator and convince him or her to vote a certain way.

Membership can also affect the group's influence. Obviously, membership in interest groups vary. Groups with large memberships are often more effective than those with small membership simply because they have more people who can demonstrate, keep an issue alive, or make it a public issue (by drawing attention to it). Legislators find it difficult to turn away large numbers of people (Ripley 1983).

Leadership can also determine how effective a group will be. Leadership in interest groups is usually elected, and it becomes part of the internal hierarchy of administration. Knowledge of other groups is important to the effectiveness of groups. Through contacts, watchdog activity, visible or secret liaison agents, public relations units, or representatives on advisory boards or commissions can provide information about other groups' activities.

Interest groups can be divided into consumer groups and secondary groups. Consumer groups are those whose members are directly affected by the policy. This would include police organizations, the fraternal order of police or lawyers groups like the American Bar Association (ABA). Secondary groups are those whose members are interested in the policy but are not directly affected by it. For example, the American Civil Liberties Union (ACLU) is active in many issues surrounding criminal justice for those accused or convicted of committing crimes (Steel and Steger 1988, 92).

No matter what types of groups they are, the groups are educating the public about political issues (Berry 1984). The groups provide information about the problem at hand and possible solutions. In doing so, the groups can help build the government's agenda (Berry 1984). In this sense, interest groups are a link between citizens and government.

Interest Groups and the Courts

Interest groups often become involved in court cases to enact social change. They will usually choose cases that reflect broad constitutional questions (Glick 1993, 189). Not only can they take these test cases to court, but they can also file *amicus curiae* (friends of the court) briefs that provide a legal arguments for one side of the case (Daynes 1988, 61).

Groups likely to use test cases are the American Civil Liberties Union (ACLU), the American Liberty League, and the Mountain States Legal Foundation, which goes to court on behalf of businesses and other groups who favor greater use of public lands for mining, oil drilling, and other commercial ventures (Glick 1993, 197). The American Bar Association (ABA) is also very involved in court issues. The ABA usually evaluates nominees to the courts after the president has nominated them. They prefer to evaluate nominees before they are nominated so the group does not have to oppose a nominee (Edwards and Wayne 1985). For example, it was involved in the nomination of Judge Bork to the Supreme Court, whom it rated as "well qualified" (O'Brien 1993, 115).

Criminal Justice Interest Groups

There has been very little research on interest groups in criminal justice (Fairchild 1981, 182). One reason for the lack of research is that crime was not a federal issue until relatively recently. But when crime shifted to the federal level, some powerful interest groups got involved, including groups such as the ABA and the ACLU (Hallett and Palumbo 1993, xiv). This opened the way for other groups to join and become involved in the process.

Below is a sampling of interest groups active in attempting to influence criminal justice policies. Criminal justice interest groups are "organizations that are entirely or partially dedicated to influencing the formulation and execution of public policy in the areas of crime and criminal justice administration" (Fairchild 1981, 183). There are many more groups involved in criminal justice than those listed here. Some groups that would not normally be considered a criminal justice group can have a significant impact on legislation. For example, the National Organization for Women (NOW), an interest group not focused solely on crime policy, influenced the definition of domestic violence (Hallett and Palumbo 1993, xvii). Such groups are concerned with criminal justice issues only sporadically.

NATIONAL RIFLEMAN'S ASSOCIATION (NRA)

The National Rifleman's Association, or NRA, was established in 1871 and has as its primary purpose "to protect and defend the Constitution of the U.S., especially with reference to the inalienable right of the individual American citizen guaranteed by such Constitution to acquire, possess, transport, carry, transfer ownership of, and enjoy the right to use arms, in order that the people may always be in a position to exercise their legitimate individual right of self preservation and defense of family, person, and property, as well as to serve effectively in the appropriate militia for the common defense of the Republic and the individual liberty of its citizens." Some secondary purposes are to promote public safety, to train members of law enforcement agencies, the armed forces, the militia and people of good repute, to foster and promote the shooting sports, and to promote hunter safety.

The NRA has a paid staff of 390 and its 1987 budget was $50 million. Dues made up about 85% of that money, but they also received over $15 million in contributions from its membership, which is 2.8 million (13,000 clubs). Overall, the NRA gave $4.7 million to campaigns in 1985-86. The NRA also becomes involved in the legislative process by lobbying with telephone calls to legislators, radio spots that highlight an issue, and media coverage of issues and legislators' positions (Loftus 1994).

The NRA also has an Institute for Legislative Action, which was created in 1982. The Institute reported spending $450,737 on lobbying (Spitzer 1988 p. 115). They also have the NRA Political Action Committee (PAC) called the Political Victory Fund, which spent $1.5 million in congressional campaign contributions in 1980 (Spitzer 1988, 115). In the congressional elections in 1983-84 and in senatorial elections during the 1979-84 period, the NRA PAC spent a total $1,469,865 on direct contributions to and independent expenditures on behalf of congresspersons (Spitzer 1988, 115). Most of the money goes to Republicans (Spitzer 1988, 116).

HANDGUN CONTROL, INC.

Handgun Control, Inc., was established in 1974 by citizens who wanted to "restrict, but not ban, the ownership of pistols and revolvers (in particular Saturday night specials)" (Spitzer 1988, 119). The members have lobbied Congress for legislation to control the ownership of handguns as well as for legislation to place restrictions on the manufacture and sale of firearms. In 1980 Handgun Control, Inc. gave $75,000 to campaigns, and in 1986 it gave $325,000.

Handgun Control, Inc. operates with a staff of 23 and a membership of 1 million (Spitzer 1988, 119). Its 1987 budget was $3.6 million, which rose to $7 million recently (Hallett and Palumbo 1993, 37). Dues and contributions make up 98% of this.

CITIZENS COMMITTEE FOR THE RIGHT TO KEEP AND BEAR ARMS

CCRKBA, founded in 1971 and composed of nearly 600,000 members, is a national grassroots lobbying organization that is dedicated to the defense of the Second Amendment right to keep and bear arms. They are an anti-gun control group that works to ensure that restrictive firearms legislation does not become law. Their staff includes a director, three senior attorneys, three staff attorneys, a publications director, and three support staff. They also have 650,000 members and a budget of over $2.5 million (Hallett and Palumbo 1993, 22). The group provides education activities at seminars, conferences, schools, and gunshows, and provides literature for television and radio. They also have a political victory fund to work towards electing pro-gun legislators to office. The group sponsors a gun rights policy conference that provides a forum where national strategies and agendas can be formulated. The group provides a publication to their members called *Point Blank*.

THE COALITION TO STOP GUN VIOLENCE

The Coalition to Stop Gun Violence was founded in 1974 with the purpose of banning the sale of handguns and assault weapons to private individuals. Its ultimate goal is the orderly elimination of most handguns from society, with exceptions including the police, military, security officers and gun clubs. They also support waiting periods and background checks for weapons purchases and removing from circulation small handguns known as Saturday night specials. They are a coalition of 34 national organizations, including religious, professional, labor, medical, and educational associations.

They have an Education Fund to End Handgun Violence, founded in 1978 as a non-profit educational charity dedicated to ending violence caused by the use of firearms, particularly as it affects children. As part of this, they have initiated research into firearms violence, a monitoring of the firearms industry, public education, and a firearms litigation clearinghouse. The clearinghouse has a comprehensive library of firearms litigation. The clearinghouse also provides legal assistance to victims and their attorneys in terms of case law, depositions, patents, government tests and recalls.

NOVA: NATIONAL ORGANIZATION FOR VICTIM ASSISTANCE

NOVA was founded 1975 by people who had been working with victims of crime in rape crisis centers, domestic violence shelters, prosecutors' offices, law enforcement agencies, and community-based organizations. The 1989 membership of the groups was 3,600, and has grown to a current membership of 4,500. During the 1980s, the staff for NOVA consisted in nine people, who controlled a budget of over $1 million (Hallett and Palumbo 1993, 77).

NOVA has national advocacy activities where it lobbies for victim interests in legislative and executive branches of government. They realize that victims need help, whether it be financial, medical, or emotional. Therefore, they provide direct services to victims of crime including crisis intervention, shelter, clothing, emergency aid, help with filling out insurance forms or victim compensation forms, or services to keep the victim informed of the investigation and arrest, assistance in the court appearance (transportation child care, counseling) and pre- and post-sentence counseling. They also provide technical assistance and training: helping local victim assistance programs expand their programs.

This group claims their success in many ways. First they point out that in 1980 there were 27 victim compensation programs in the U.S., but in 1989 this number had grown to 46. The group also states that in 1980, only a few jurisdictions took into consideration the impact of the crime on the victim when determining the offender's sentence, but in 1989, 48 states allowed or required victim input at sentencing. Further, NOVA also points out that in 1980 the concept of "victim rights" was only a concept, and in 1989, 45 states had a bill of rights for crime victims. In addition, as of 1980, no president had ever taken a leadership role on behalf of victims, but President Reagan proclaimed a National Victim's Week eight times. Each of these activities, NOVA claims, is evidence of NOVA's success in bringing the plight of victims to the attention of the nation.

NATIONAL ASSOCIATION OF CRIME VICTIM COMPENSATION BOARDS

The membership of this group is limited to agencies that operate compensation programs that provide financial assistance to victims of violent crime. They have national and regional training conferences, a quarterly newsletter to promote and exchange ideas and information among the state programs. They also serve as a liaison to the federal government.

NATIONAL CENTER FOR PROSECUTION OF CHILD ABUSE

The National Center for Prosecution of Child Abuse was created in 1985 by the National District Attorneys Association with a goal of providing technical assistance and training to child abuse prosecutors and professionals. They provide training, expert legal assistance, court reform and state-of-the-art information on criminal child abuse investigations and prosecutions. They also provide research on state and federal developments, and parental abduction of children. The group publishes a number publications and newsletters for its members and the general public.

HALT: AN ORGANIZATION OF AMERICANS FOR LEGAL REFORM

HALT was established in 1978 with a goal of reforming the

legal system. The organization now has a membership of 160,000, most of whom are lawyers. The members of HALT want to make the American legal system more fair, simple, and accessible to all people. To do this, they offer alternatives to litigation through methods such as mediation or small claims courts, and also support methods to simplify the court system and open it up to non-lawyers. For example, they provide standard, do-it-yourself forms and booklets that "walk" non-lawyers through the legal process and allow them to avoid legal costs. The emphasis is on self-representation and mediation rather than upon a reliance on lawyers and court hearings. The members also support effective lawyer discipline. To do this, HALT has a staff of 23, with a 1987 budget of $2.3 million.

ABA: The American Bar Association

The ABA is the foremost national professional organization in the nation that represents attorneys. The group has effective leadership and an extremely high status reputation with the general public. The group is very active and influential, often testifying in congressional hearings or in the nomination process of potential justices. They consider themselves to be impartial or objective experts who can aid legislators in either creating fair legislation or appointing qualified persons to the judiciary. Their lawyers do not necessarily support an ideological position, but rather are concerned with inconsistencies, ambiguities and out-dated provisions of statutes (Steel and Steger 1988, 95).

The American Bar Association has a section of criminal justice, referred to as the ABA-SCJ. This is made up of prosecutors, defense lawyers, judges, academics, correctional personnel, and other experts who work in the field but are not lawyers. It has a staff of ten and a budget of over $750,000. The ABA-SCJ has been active with regard to the application of the death penalty for juveniles, the 1988 Anti-Drug Abuse Act, and the development of procedural guidelines and standards for the courts. The ABA-SCJ supports gun control, sentencing reform legislation, limits on federal habeas corpus appeals in death penalty cases, and the exclusionary rule. It opposes mandatory minimum sentences.

National Associations of Attorneys General

The NAAG was founded in 1907 to help attorneys general

fulfill the responsibilities of their office and to assure the provision of high quality legal services to the states. The agency supports interstate cooperation on legal and law enforcement issues, conducts policy research and analysis of issues, and facilitates communication between the states' chief legal officers and all levels of government. Among the goals of the agency are:

1. To produce information related to the independence, scope, and management of the office of the attorney general;

2. To create and maintain a network among attorney generals;

3. To promote cooperation on interstate legal matters

4. To advise Attorneys General about legislative or legal developments;

5. To increase citizen understanding of the law and law enforcement's role; and

6. To influence the development of national and state legal policy.

NAAG's members include the attorneys general of the states and the chief legal officer of the District of Columbia and territories. The U.S. attorney general is an honorary member. There are seven standing committees that focus on particular areas, including antitrust, civil rights, consumer protection, criminal law, environment and energy, insurance, and Supreme Court. They also have special committees as needed. NAAG provides services to its members, including legal research assistance, seminars and reports.

FEDERAL BAR ASSOCIATION

The Federal Bar Association is made up of interested people who have been admitted to the practice of law before a federal court or court of record in a U.S. state or territory. They also have law student and foreign associate members. The Federal Bar Association has a number of sections, including, among others, administration of justice, antitrust and trade regulation, bankruptcy law, federal litigation, government contracts, Indian law, and international law. The divisions include federal career service, judiciary, senior lawyers, younger lawyers, state and local government relations, taxation, transportation law and veterans law.

THE SENTENCING PROJECT

The Sentencing Project is a non profit organization established 1986 with a goal of developing sentencing programs designed to promote alternatives to incarceration, and to improve the sentencing of indigent defendants. The members are concerned with the high number of people serving time in correctional facilities, and see the need to reduce prison overcrowding. Overall, the members want to help create a more rational and effective crime policy and criminal justice system. To meet this goal, the group has sponsored training programs for judges to provide information and ideas on sentencing of drug offenders, alternative sentencing, published information documenting incarceration rates, information on the issues of race in criminal justice system, trained legal staff in the New York Legal Aid Society, established a network of alternative sentencing programs in Alabama, and evaluated community corrections programs in New York state. They were also involved with the formation of the National Association of Sentencing Advocates, the first professional organization devoted to the needs of sentencing advocates. The Sentencing Project claims to have helped the courts, policymakers, and the public in their understanding of crime and punishment issues.

NATIONAL CENTER ON INSTITUTIONS AND ALTERNATIVES

The National Center on Institutions and Alternatives is a private, nonprofit agency that provides training, technical assistance, research and direct services to criminal justice, juvenile justice, social service, and mental health organizations. It was created in 1977 and is involved with planning and needs assessment to jurisdictions facing institutional overcrowding, alternative sentencing and placements, community reintegration of offenders, design and administration of institutions for serious, juvenile offenders, alternative programs for violators of probation and parole, mental health counseling for sex offenders and victims,and research and consultation on jail suicide programs.

Since 1979, the agency has worked primarily in providing sentencing assistance to federal and state courts. It provides the courts with detailed, individualized sentencing options for primarily felony offenders who would normally be incarcerated.

NATIONAL ASSOCIATION OF CHIEFS OF POLICE

The NACP is a non profit national association of law enforcement supervisory professionals. They provide training programs, employment assistance, a program of awards for service and valor for favorable activities, and a $10,000 benefit for any crime related death. They also publish *The Chief of Police* to disseminate information about issues that would concern people that work in the profession.

FRATERNAL ORDER OF POLICE (FOP)

The FOP was originally founded in 1915 and is currently the nation's largest law enforcement organization with over 230,000 members and an annual budget of over $1 million. The FOP is active in issues related to police and law enforcement, such as wages, benefits, and pensions.

NATIONAL ORGANIZATION FOR THE REFORM OF MARIJUANA LAWS

NORML is the oldest and largest national agency that focuses only on marijuana law reform. It was formed in 1970 as a non profit agency to educate the public and lobby legislators for a "more reasonable" approach to the use of marijuana. Stating that the current laws against marijuana are unjust, NORML asks legislators to remove all penalties for marijuana use by adults. They state that Americans have spent billions of dollars to arrest over 9 million Americans since 1965. They also argue that there are many medical uses of marijuana, including for patients of cancer, glaucoma, MS and epilepsy. They even point to industrial and environmental benefits to the drug.

NORML has almost 100 local chapters across the nation and a national office in Washington, D.C. The national office acts as an information clearinghouse and disseminates information for members, the media and the public. It relies mostly on dues and contributions for its support.

Members of NORML do not advocate marijuana use, but rather the adult's right to choose. NORML advocates the removal

of all penalties for the private possession of marijuana, cultivation for personal use, and casual non profit transfers of small
amounts. They also advocate regulation and taxation of large
amounts of cultivation and distribution. They also advocate
abolishing urine tests for detecting marijuana use, replacing
them with tests to detect present impairment.

DPF: THE DRUG POLICY FOUNDATION

The members of the Drug Policy Foundation include professionals and citizens who want to reform drug policies. The group
was established in 1987 by academics, corporate executives, and
private citizens in both the U.S. and abroad. They are a non profit
independent organization with a full-time staff of 14 and a
membership of over 5,000 (Hallett and Palumbo 1993, 29). The
group promotes alternatives to the current drug policies including legalization of marijuana, decriminalization of possession of
controlled substances, the ability to use marijuana and heroin for
medical use, and needle exchange programs in inner cities (Hallett and Palumbo 1993, 29). They serve to educate the public in
these issues by publishing *The Drug Policy Letter*.

NCARL: NATIONAL COMMITTEE AGAINST REPRESSIVE LEGISLATION

The National Committee Against Repressive Legislation acts
to protect Americans' constitutional liberties. The members of
NCARL believe that presidents and the government make policies that suppress dissent and control information to the public,
and providing the public with distortions and falsifications. They
fight against the abuses of executive power and promote policies
which lead to the expansion of political rights for Americans.
They claim that scientists are prohibited from publishing important information about their findings, that the FBI is allowed to
use intrusive surveillance means to collect information on people,
that "whistle blowers" are not able to come forward and charge
abuse, and that presidents, through executive order, can classify
documents or reclassify documents as secret, curtailing the
Freedom of Information Act.

NCARL was originally founded as the National Committee to
Abolish the House Un-American Activities Committee. This was
in response to the committee's and FBI director Hoover's alleged
obliteration of the Bill of Rights. They were involved with repeal-

ing the federal "No Knock" legislation, which violated the Fourth Amendment, and fought against the Federal Criminal Code revision which passed in 1984, claiming it was repressive and eroded due process rights.

NATIONAL ASSOCIATION OF CRIMINAL JUSTICE PLANNERS

This group was formed in 1971 as a professional agency formed to improve planning in the criminal justice system. It provides information to federal, state and local criminal justice officials for use in planning, program development, and resource allocation, as well as provides information to elected officials in identifying solutions and attempting to make federal policy more responsive to the needs of cities, counties, and other local governments. With a membership of over 180 individuals and agencies, they can share information on programs and policies that have been effective. The group has recognized four purposes:

1. To conduct research, surveys, conferences and educational activities that enhance the public's understanding of criminal justice and the forces that affect criminal justice operations;

2. To provide informational assistance to all persons and organizations involved in the criminal justice system;

3. To support the continuing development and implementation of standards to improve criminal justice; and

4. To improve the professional development of criminal justice planners.

Conclusion

Interest groups provide another example of the complex relationship between political science institutions and the criminal justice system. These groups have the power or the ability to influence legislation through many techniques, including lobbying, providing testimony about a bill, or educating the public about a particular issue. The agencies listed above provide only a sampling of the groups involved with the political aspect of criminal justice issues.

Bibliography

Berry, J.M. 1984. *The Interest Group Society*. Boston: Little, Brown and Company.

Biskupic, J. 1991. "Letter-Writing and Campaigns." *Congressional Quarterly Weekly Report* 49: 183.

Davidson, R.H. and W.J. Oleszek. 1985. *Congress and Its Members*. Washington, D.C.: CQ Press.

Daynes, B.W. 1988. "Pornography: Freedom of Expression or Societal Degradation?" In R. Tatalovich and B.W. Daynes (Eds.), *Social Regulatory Policy*. Boulder: Westview Press.

Edwards, G.C. III and S.J. Wayne. 1985. *Presidential Leadership* New York: St. Martin's Press.

Eagleton, T.F. 1991. *Issues in Business and Government*. Englewood Cliffs, New Jersey: Prentice Hall.

Fairchild, E. 1981. "Interest Groups in the Criminal Justice Process." *Journal of Criminal Justice* 9: 181-194.

Glick, H.R. 1993. *Courts, Politics and Justice*. New York: McGraw Hill, Inc.

Hallett, M.A. and D.J. Palumbo. 1993. *U.S. Criminal Justice Interest Groups*. Westport, Conn: Greenwood Press.

Hamilton, A., J. Jay, and J. Madison. 1961. *The Federalist Papers*. C. Rossiter (Ed.), New York: New American Library.

Key, V.O., Jr. 1990. "Pressure Groups." In Peter Woll (Ed.), *American Government: Readings and Cases*. Glenview, Illinois: Scott, Foresman and Company.

Loftus, T. 1994. *The Art of Legislative Politics*. Washington, D.C.: CQ Press.

Melone, A.P. and R. Slagter. 1983. "Interest Group Politics and the Reform of the Federal Criminal Code." In S. Nagel, E. Fairchild and A. Champagne (Eds.), *The Political Science of Criminal Justice*. Springfield, Illinois: Charles C. Thomas, Publisher.

O'Brien, D.M. 1993. *Storm Center*. New York: W.W. Norton and Company.

Ripley, R.B. 1983. *Congress: Process and Policy*. New York: W.W. Norton and Company.

Schlozman, K.L. and J.T. Tierney. 1993. "More of the Same: Washington Pressure Group Activity in a Decade of Change." In R.B. Ripley and E.E. Slotnik (Eds.), *Readings in American Government*. Belmont, CA: Wadsworth Publishing Company.

Spitzer, R.J. 1988. "Gun Control: Constitutional Mandate or Myth?" in R. Tatalovich and B.W. Daynes (Eds.), *Social Regulatory Policy*. Boulder: Westview Press.

Steel, B.S. and M.A.E. Steger. 1988. "Crime: Due Process Liberalism Versus Law-and-Order Conservatism." in R. Tatalovich and B.W. Daynes (Eds.), *Social Regulatory Policy*. Boulder: Westview Press.
Wittenberg, E. and E. Wittenberg. 1990. *How to Win in Washington*. Cambridge, MA: Basil Blackwell, Inc.

Seven

Campaigns, Elections, and the Issue of Crime

WHEN PEOPLE THINK of elections and campaigns, they rarely consider crime as an issue that can impact the outcomes of presidential races. But many campaigns have been at least influenced by a candidate's position on crime issues. As an election concern, crime was not a significant factor until the mid 1960s (Rosch 1985, 20). But since then, crime continues to play an important role in the political realm of elections.

The issue of crime is a "safe" issue for candidates, one that will not evoke much disagreement from voters (Rosch 1985, 20; Jacob et al. 1982, 3). It is safe to assume that most people will be against a rise in the crime rate, and will support an anti-crime and violence platform. Most politicians will be able to obtain support from voters by taking an anti-crime stance. However, the crime issue can have negative long-term implications for candidates and elected officials because in all likelihood, candidates will be forced to make promises that they will not be able to keep, and crime will not respond to policies enacted by the legislators (Scheingold 1984, 76). Once in office there is no guarantee that the official will pursue the campaign promises made about crime (Scheingold 1984, 77).

Campaign issues can be divided into two types: substantive or positional issues versus personal or valence issues. The first, substantive issues, are those that have two sides and a candidate must choose one position or another. In this case, candidates must persuade voters that their position, or side, is the right one. An example of this is school prayer: either people are for or against it. The second type of issue is a personal, or valence, issue. These are issues in which everyone is supportive and not opposed. These are issues such as leadership, compassion, or empathy. No one would be against effective leadership. In this case, candidates vie to demonstrate to the voters that they are the more trustworthy or able candidate (Salmore and Salmore 1985, 117).

Crime control is an interesting issue in that it can be labelled as both a positional and a valence issue. There are two sides to many sub-issues in criminal justice. Candidates can be for or against the death penalty. Or for or against an assault weapons ban. Or for or against decriminalizing marijuana laws. However, no candidate will support policies to increase crime. Every candidate will be for crime control in some sense. So the issue is a valence issue since every candidate is against it, and voters have to decide which candidate is better able to solve the problem based on his or her honesty and integrity. But it is a positional issue because there are definite sides to many issues within the broad area called criminal justice.

It is possible that two candidates in a campaign will choose the valence issue of crime control as a theme, but each one will have different positions on that problem (Salmore and Salmore 1985, 125). Voters must then choose which candidate's position on the issues will be more effective.

Beyond being a valence and a positional issue in elections, crime also acts as a symbolic issue because the "politicians do their best to conceal what is really at stake" (Scheingold 1984, 84). Candidates do not discuss the complexity of the crime problem as it is related to the limited resources available to the government

(Cronin et al. 1981, 170). For the voter, the crime problem evokes emotional concerns about his or her personal safety (Cronin et al. 1981, 5). People turn to their elected representatives for reassurance and a sense of progress and action (Barber 1986). Generally, using crime as a symbolic issue works for candidates because the majority of voters have little personal or valid information about crime, and they rely on the politician to study an issue and create effective policies (Kessel 1975).

Whether it is used as a valence, positional, or symbolic issue, crime was not used as a political issue until the 1960s. Since then, the candidates for president of the U.S. have turned to the issues of crime in various ways. Below is an analysis of the crime issues as they were used in the presidential elections since 1964 and how they played a role in the final outcomes of those elections.

1964 Presidential Election

The attention of Americans to issues surrounding crime control made crime a major campaign issue for the first time in the 1964 presidential election (Rosch 1985, 20). President Johnson was running for reelection on the Democratic ticket, and Barry Goldwater had received the Republican nomination. The leadership of the Republican party in 1964 believed that the public's concerns about law and order could be used as a campaign issue (Cronin et al. 1981, 18). In his acceptance speech for the nomination, Goldwater noted that the Republican party would pass policies to enforce law and order and provide freedom from domestic violence. He also told reporters that crime was the second most important issue facing the nation, behind foreign policy. Goldwater hoped that the voters would support a candidate who promised to reestablish local law and order.

Goldwater used FBI statistics to demonstrate that crime had increased in the nation during previous Democratic administrations. He claimed the Democrats were to blame because they were weak on crime. He also claimed that the crime problem was the result of a weakened morality and a decline in discipline in both the nation and the Johnson administration. He believed that no social welfare problems could ever improve the nation's morality, so the criminal justice system had to become more tough, with more powerful police, tougher laws, and a less permissive court system.

At the outset of the election, the Democrats did not respond to the Republican attacks about crime control, believing that it was not a major campaign issue. When he finally did respond to Goldwater's attacks, Johnson explained that the increase in crime was the result of social and economic decay that resulted from unemployment, poverty, and inflation. He argued that his "Great Society" policies directed at eliminating or reducing the social problems would also affect the crime rate ("Responsibility for Rising Crime Rates..." 1964). Johnson did not spend as much time on crime as did his opponent, and never offered any specific policies to stop crime. On the whole, Democrats were not able to use the issue as well as the Republicans (Rosch 1985, 27).

Although the crime debate did not entirely alter the outcome of the election, this election helped to define the role of the federal government with regard to crime control. "The issue of crime was seized and expanded and given a national focus by candidate Goldwater" (Cronin et al. 1981, 23). Goldwater was able to set the scene for a national debate about crime (Rosch 1985, 25). This election may have also resulted in an increase in federal activity with regard to crime control. Where it had previously been viewed as a states' rights issue, crime was becoming a federal issue.

1968 Presidential Election

In 1968, Americans witnessed the assassinations of Dr. Martin Luther King, Jr. and Robert F. Kennedy, as well as riots and protests against American involvement in the Vietnam War. The previous presidential campaign had set the tone about the extent of crime and social unrest in the nation, and the federal government's response to it. Crime continued to rise at a faster pace than the population (Gould 1993, 15), and public opinion polls showed that crime was the top domestic issue facing the nation that needed attention (Cronin et al. 1981, 60). Congressional members also reported that riots and crime were the top concerns of their constituents ("Johnson, GOP vie..").

Richard Nixon, the Republican candidate for president, responded to these events and the general topic of crime with a "get tough" approach. He promised to bring an end to social unrest by passing "law and order" policies. His attention to crime became a prominent election issue. Like Goldwater in the previous election, Nixon blamed the increased crime problems on the failed policies of the previous Democratic activities. "The present administration has... ignored the danger signals of our rising crime rates until very recently and... has proposed only narrow measures hopelessly inadequate to the need" ("Complete Text" 1968, 987). He stated that during the previous Democratic administrations, "we didn't have strong enough law enforcement officials; we didn't have strong enough laws; we didn't have, in my opinion, strong enough judges in many areas - judges who, as far as their records were concerned, clearly realized that it was important to strengthen the peace forces as against the criminal forces in this country" ("Remarks" 1970, 1011). Nixon claimed that the courts under the Johnson administration had failed the American public by giving too many rights to offenders at the cost to society ("NIXON" 1988; Gould 1993, 15).

Hubert Humphrey, the Democratic candidate, served as mayor of Minneapolis from 1945-1945. He was perceived to be an effective anti-crime mayor who was successful at driving organized crime from the city (Scammon and Wattenberg 1970, 167). Humphrey agreed with President Johnson that the policies incorporated in the Great Society social programs were the most effective way to address crime. Voters, who were concerned with victimization, wanted immediate solutions rather than long-term social solutions, and were beginning to wonder if these proposals were viable (Cronin et al. 1981, 63).

Officials organizing the Democratic presidential convention in Chicago that year had received threats of strikes, protests and unrest, and responded by putting up chain link and barbed wire fences. They also placed twelve thousand police officers on twelve hour shifts, as well as fifty-six hundred national guardsmen and seventy-five hundred army troops to protect the conventioneers (Cronin et al. 1981, 65). Police and demonstrators clashed the night Humphrey was nominated, and television units broadcast the riots across the nation. To some voters, this showed that the Democrats could not solve crime in the nation since they could not even control crime at their own convention (Cronin et al. 1981,

67).

A third candidate in this election was George Wallace, the Democratic governor of Alabama, who was running as the candidate from the American Independent Party. Law and order had always been one of his main planks. He spoke very positively of police, but felt that they needed more power to do their jobs effectively (Cronin et al. 1981, 70).

Nixon was able to appeal to the public with his law and order promises. The voters wanted action, and they felt that the Republicans could provide that action. The Democratic party members were torn about the issue of crime. They knew that the public wanted tough policies and approaches, but wanted to maintain the social welfare programs that had their basis in the Kennedy and Johnson administrations. Because of the events at the Democratic convention, many voters believed that the Democrats were not able to stop crime. Republicans, conversely, had a more cohesive approach to the problem. Although neither party really knew how to solve crime, the Republicans came across as more decisive, and Nixon won the election by half a million votes (Cronin et al. 1981, 73).

1972 Presidential Election

Despite Nixon's campaign promises in the 1968 campaign to reduce crime, the crime rate in the country during his first term did not decline. In fact, it rose 30 percent while Nixon was president ("Crime:Again a Presidential..."). The Democrats and their nominee George McGovern, used this to accuse Nixon as being "soft on crime" and of being "long on tough talk [and] short on performance" ("Crime: Again a Presidential..."). McGovern said: "There has been no major effort to make the basic change and improvement in correctional facilities that is the precondition for eliminating a high proportion of repeater crime. There is no major new effort on the part of the administration to secure better gun control, to develop policy-community relations programs, to professionalize and educate police" ("Crime" 1972, 2221). McGovern went so far as to accuse Nixon's attorney general, John Mitchell, of tampering with the FBI's reporting of crime figures and of pressuring police departments to falsify their crime figures in order to make the administration's crime fight look successful ("Crime: Again a Presidential.."). The Democratic delegates to the convention did not seem to understand or represent public opinion about crime. "On law and order, over three-fourths of the delegates cared more about the rights of the accused, compared to one-third of the voters" (Polsby and Wildavsky 1980, 144).

Nixon responded to the attack by pointing to the federal grant money that had been provided to the states during his first term. He pointed out the importance of the aid provided by the federal government to the states, saying the funds used to fight crime in the country were well spent. He pointed out that while total crime increased, the rate of increase was slowed ("Crime: Again a Presidential..."). He also described that during his first term in office, the federal government's law enforcement budget tripled from 1969; and federal aid to state and local law enforcement rose from $60 million to almost $700 million. As a result, Nixon predicted that the crime rate would soon be dropping, despite statistics from the FBI which indicated otherwise.

During the 1972 campaign, the democrats were not able to convince the voters that their anti-crime policies would work, and Nixon was re-elected to the presidency.

1976 Presidential Election

The election of 1976 was less of an issues election than elections of previous years (Cronin et al. 1981, 118). Democratic and Republican advisors decided to "tone down the issues and seek the center" (Cronin et al. 1981, 118). Both parties knew by this time (because of Nixon's campaign promises) that any promises to decrease criminal behavior probably would not be carried out, and was a risky campaign tactic (Cronin et al. 1981, 118). Both candidates agreed that the nation needed a tougher approach to crime, including mandatory minimum sentences, victim compensation, and more efficient courts (Cronin et al. 1981, 119).

Ford supported victims' rights rather than a focus only on the offender. He was wary of a strong federal government role in crime control. The Democratic candidate, Jimmy Carter, sought to reduce crime by reducing unemployment. At one point he charged the Nixon administration of not reversing the crime trends. Carter was better able to convince voters that the Democrats could effectively fight crime, and he won the election that year.

1980 Presidential Election

The election of 1980 saw the incumbent Democratic president Jimmy Carter campaigning against the Republican candidate Ronald Reagan. Once again, the challenger used the issue of crime against the incumbent. Reagan accused the Carter administration of enacting policies that were ineffective in the fight against crime. "In recent years, a murderous epidemic of drug abuse has swept our country. Carter, through his policies and his personnel, has demonstrated little interest in stopping its ravages." Reagan, of course, implied that his administration, if elected, would be successful in decreasing crime, despite being a task that no other president had been able to accomplish. Both parties in the 1980 election agreed on the issues concerning financial support for fighting crime (Polsby and Wildavsky 1980, 147).

Reagan successfully used crime and other issues to win the election, including inflation, the budget deficit, and national defense (Cronin et al. 1981, 131). Once again, there was a conservative Republican elected to office who pursued conservative anti-crime policies.

1984 Presidential Campaign

In 1984, Republican incumbent President Ronald Reagan was running for the presidency against Democratic challenger Walter Mondale. In that election, Reagan accused the Democrats in Congress of blocking crime legislation ("Reagan makes Crime..."). During his first term in office, Reagan supported the death penalty for some crimes, a restriction on the court appeals available to federal prisoners, preventive detention of dangerous suspects, and tougher penalties for drug offenders. "In 1984, the Republican party again made clear its opposition to pornography; the party platform stated that 'the Republican Party has deep concern about gratuitous sex and violence in the entertainment media, both of which contribute to the problem of crime against children and women'" (Daynes 1988, 52). Reagan also supported the anti-pornography platform.

The democratic candidate Mondale barely mentioned crime during the course of his campaign. He felt it was more appropriate for members of Congress to respond to Republican accusations about blocking anti-crime legislation than to respond to the charges himself ("Reagan makes Crime..."). Mondale supported the creation of a "drug czar" position to be a centralized anti-drug official. He also supported restricting U.S. aid to nations that were not active in the fight against drug smuggling. Finally, candidate Mondale did not support the death penalty.

The American public that year reelected the conservative candidate. This gave Reagan another term as president to pursue his conservative anti-crime agenda.

1988 Presidential Campaign

George Bush, who was vice president for eight years under Ronald Reagan, ran for president in 1988 against Michael Dukakis, then-governor of Massachusetts. Crime played a significant role in that election in many ways. First, during a debate between the two candidates, CNN anchorman Bernard Shaw presented Dukakis with a hypothetical situation where his wife, Kitty, was raped and murdered. Shaw asked Dukakis if he would favor an irrevocable death penalty for the killer. Dukakis showed little emotion when answering, and did not even mention his wife's name. He said he would not support the death penalty because in his view, the death penalty is not a deterrent. He then continued on a tangent about drug treatment programs (Kessel 1992, 238; Pomper 1989, 94). George Bush used this against Dukakis. He implied that Dukakis would support policies that would be ineffective in reducing crime.

Second, Bush and his advisors discovered that a murder-rapist from Massachusetts, Willie Horton, had stabbed a man and raped his fiancée while on furlough (Kessel 1992). Bush placed the blame for Horton's crime spree on Dukakis, who tried to point out that the furlough program in Massachusetts had its origins under a previous Republican governor, and that there were similar stories in programs under both Reagan and Bush. But Dukakis was unable to counter the attack. He said the furlough programs were quite common (Kessel 1992, 229). This event furthered Bush's allegations that Dukakis was weak in the fight against crime (Pomper 1989, 73, 86).

The Democrats accused the Republicans of using the Horton issue to inflame the nation's racial fears as Horton was black and his victim white. They also tried to show that the administration was weak on crime. As evidence, they pointed to the lack of results from the "Just Say No" anti-drug program, and to the lack of action with Panama's drug kingpin Noriega (Pomper 1989, 190). Bush responded to the criticisms by saying that Horton symbolized the "misguided" outlook that Dukakis had about crime (Rosenthal 1988).

Third, Bush also accused Dukakis of being a "card carrying member of the ACLU" during the campaign. The Bush campaign used Dukakis' ACLU membership to label him an extremist liberal who, because he was a member of the organization, supported child pornography, the Ku Klux Klan (KKK), and was soft on crime. Dukakis never responded to these attacks, which implied that there was something to hide about his affiliation with the group. Experts noted that Dukakis could have removed himself from the attacks by pointing out that the ACLU had taken his administration to court over violations of civil liberties (Walker 1990, 368-9).

On the whole, Bush was able to use crime related issues to his advantage during this campaign against Dukakis, and he was successfully elected into office to replace Reagan and serve as President for four years.

1992 Presidential Election

In 1992, Democrat Bill Clinton ran for the presidency against George Bush, the Republican incumbent president seeking re-election. Crime played only a minor role in this election because it was overshadowed by economic concerns. The issues of crime remained a concern to American citizens, but it was temporarily second to other worries.

Bush tried to make crime an issue as he did in the 1988

election, but he was not successful. Voters remembered Bush's
promises made in the 1988 election to reduce crime, and they
realized that Bush was not successful in following up on his
promises to reduce crime. In addition, Bush attempted to charac-
terize Clinton as being a "soft on crime" Democrat. Clinton,
however, was more conservative in his suggested crime control
initiatives. Bush's strategy, therefore, was not beneficial to his
campaign.

President Bush supported the death penalty, especially for
drug kingpins, killers of law enforcement officers, and terrorists.
He supported the reduction of habeas corpus appeals that allow
inmates to appeal their sentences. As a sportsman and lifelong
member of the NRA, Bush was opposed to a national registration
of handguns and to a federal ban on domestic manufacture and
distribution of assault weapons. However, he did support the
Brady Bill and mandatory minimum sentences for felons possess-
ing firearms. With regard to the prison system, Bush supported
increased funding for prisons and opposed early release of criminals because of overcrowding. Finally, Bush wanted to strength-
en the laws dealing with sexual and domestic violence, cracking
down on gang violence, and protecting elderly Americans.

Clinton supported the death penalty, especially for those who
killed law enforcement officers, for multiple murderers, or for
drug kingpins. He emphasized the need to increase the number
of police officers on the streets, and even proposed a federal police
corps where college graduates could serve as law enforcement
officers to pay back student loans. The Brady bill was a major
concern to Clinton, which involved a waiting period for the
purchase of handguns until automated records were created to
check the criminal history and mental health history of people
purchasing guns. Clinton favored non-prison alternatives for
younger and least-violent offenders, and boot camps for first time
offenders. Finally, Clinton supported drug treatment programs
to help drug abusers stop their behaviors.

Despite Bush's strong anti-crime rhetoric, he was not able to
win reelection to the presidency. For the first time in twelve
years, Americans elected a Democrat to serve as president.

Conclusion

The issues of crime control have recently become part of the campaign scene in America, and can have major impact on the outcomes of those campaigns. Crime and the proper treatment of criminals are issues that have not gone away (Elshtain 1989, p. 119), and probably will not in the near future. Criminal behavior is a major concern of voters who demand action by legislators once in office. Crime as an issue in campaigns provides one more example of the increased role of criminal justice issues in politics, and of the fact that the two issues are so intertwined.

Bibliography

Barber, J.D. 1986. "The Presidency: What Americans Want." In P.S. Novola and D.H. Rosenbloom (Eds.), *Classic Readings in American Politics*. New York: St. Martin's Press.

"Complete Text of the 1968 Republican Platform." 1968. *Congressional Quarterly Almanac* 24: 987-994.

"Crime." 1972. *Congressional Quarterly Weekly Report* 30: 2221.

"Crime: Again a Presidential Election Year Issue." *Congressional Quarterly Weekly Report* 30: 2323-2325.

Cronin, T.E., T.Z. Cronin, and M.Milakovich. 1981. *U.S. v. Crime in the Streets*. Bloomington: Indiana University Press.

Daynes, B.R. 1988. "Pornography: Freedom of Expression or Societal Degradation?" In R. Tatalovich and B.W. Daynes (Eds.), *Social Regulatory Policy*. Boulder: Westview Press.

Elshtain, J.B. 1989. "Issues and Themes in the 1988 Campaign." In M. Nelson (Ed.), *The Elections of 1988*. Washington, D.C.: CQ Press.

Gould, L.L. 1993. *1968: The Election that Changed America*. Chicago: Ivan R. Dee.

Jacob, H., R. Lineberry, A.M. Heinz, J.A. Beecher, J. Moran, and D.H. Swank. 1982. *Governmental Responses to Crime: Crime on Urban Agendas*. Washington, D.C.: Department of Justice, National Institute of Justice.

"Johnson, GOP Vie for Election-Year Anticrime Program." *Congressional Quarterly Weekly Report* 26: 392-394.

Kessel, J.H. 1992. *Presidential Campaign Politics*. Pacific Grove, Ca.: Brooks/Cole Publishing Company.

"Nixon." 1968. *Congressional Quarterly Weekly Report*. 26: 88.

Polsby, N.W. and A. Wildavsky. 1980. *Presidential Elections*. New York: Free Press.

Pomper, G. 1989. *The Election of 1988*. Chatham, N.J.: Chatham House Publishers, Inc.

"Reagan Makes Crime a Campaign Issue" 1984. *Congressional Quarterly Weekly Report* 42: 2451.

"Remarks Made in Omaha, Nebraska." 1970. *Public Papers of the President*, 1011-1019.

"Responsibility for Rising Crime Rates an Election Issue." 1964. *Congressional Quarterly Weekly Report* 22: 2602-2605.

Rosch, J. 1985. "Crime as an Issue in American Politics." In E. Fairchild and V.A. Webb (Eds.), *The Politics of Crime and Criminal Justice*. Beverly Hills: Sage Publications.

Rosenthal, A. 1988. "Foes Accuse Bush Campaign of Inflaming Racial Tension." *New York Times* October 24, 1988, p. A1.

Salmore, S.A. and B.G. Salmore. 1985. *Candidates, Parties and Campaigns*. Washington, D.C.: CQ Press.

Scammon, R. and B. Wattenberg. 1970. *The Real Majority*. New York: Coward-McCann.

Scheingold, S.A. 1984. *The Politics of Law and Order*. New York: Longman Inc.

Walker, S. 1990. *In Defense of American Liberties*. New York: Oxford University Press.

Eight

The Media and Public Opinion

THE MEDIA AND public opinion are both inherent parts of the legislative and political process in the United States. It is well recognized that they impact the government and that they impact each other. But few people realize that both have important influences on the criminal justice system. This chapter will discuss these relationships and demonstrate that the powers of each of these components can have enormous impact on criminal justice.

The media's impact on criminal justice occurs almost daily. The term "mass media" refers to "media that are easily, inexpensively, and simultaneously accessible to large segments of a population" (Surette 1992, 10). The media consists of print (all printed information such as newspapers, magazines, and books), and broadcast media (including television, radio, film and recordings). These make up the major source of information for most Americans. "A Roper Poll in 1984 found that 20% of Americans received most of their news from both newspapers and television, 24% from newspapers without television, and 49% from television alone" (Hellinger and Judd 1994). The media has this responsibility because it can often simplify complex issues and explain them to the public in terms they can readily understand. Because of this, people rely on the media for information about criminal behavior. Since most people have no personal, direct experience with crime, they must rely upon the media to provide them with information about the crime problem (Lewis 1981, 128).

Beyond being a primary news source, the media is also a source of entertainment. This is especially true with crime. Crime themes appear on talk shows, in advertising, in pop/rock music, in comics, and in movies (Newman 1990). Stories about crime and criminals on "info-tainment" shows such as *American Journal* or *A Current Affair* have also proliferated. In addition, there are "true crime" shows, including *Cops* and *America's Most Wanted* that receive high ratings. Documentaries such as *48 Hours* and *Prime Time Live* regularly have segments relating to criminal events or issues. The success of these shows points to the interest (or even obsession) Americans have with crime (Parenti 1992, 113).

As a source of information and entertainment, the media has a significant amount of power to influence criminal justice. This can be seen in various ways. First, the media can alter the perceptions people have of the criminal justice system (Van Horn et al. 1992, 234). Since most people rely on the media to learn about crime, they believe what they see or read in the media and form an opinion about crime policy based on that information.

However, when it comes to criminal justice, what the media shows may not reflect reality. There are many examples of distortion by the media with regard to crime. For instance, criminals on television are most often white, middle class males with a high school social status, and older than actual criminals. The typical arrestee in real life is a young, poor, black male. The victims on television are portrayed as predominantly white, mostly young women, with whites over-represented as murder victims. In actuality the average victim is a young black male. Intrafamily violence is under-represented on television, but premeditated crimes are overrepresented (Lewis 1981, 132; Surette 1992, 35; Dye et al. 1992).

The stages in the justice system as portrayed in the media are also distorted. The early steps of the process (law enforcement, investigation and arrest) are emphasized, and the other steps are almost invisible, especially informal procedures such as plea bargaining. Lawyers are often shown as actively investigating crimes, which rarely occurs. The media shows weapons that are either completely inaccurate or completely accurate - people either don't get shot or they get shot while moving far away, being killed painlessly. Most crimes are solved on television, but the clearance rate reported by the FBI is only 23%. The offenses that are emphasized by the media are those that are least likely to occur in real life. For example, property crime is under-represented and violent crime is over-represented (Surette 1992, 34). Further, the media "exaggerate[s] the most terrifying crimes and mislead[s] people into thinking of the predatory stranger as the typical criminal" (Scheingold 1984, 55). The press tends to focus on street crime, and downplay corporate crimes which may be more damaging and kill more people (Parenti 1993, 10; Steel and Steger 1988, 77).

Another way the media distorts reality is by reporting stories that are unique or very violent rather than typical crimes. When a criminal commits an unusual crime, for example the 1989 shooting of schoolchildren in Stockton, California, the media will pick up the story and publicize it. However, the usual or everyday crimes that occur most frequently, such as muggings or street crimes, are ignored. They occur too frequently to be of interest to the average American.

The unbalanced or biased presentation of crime stories by the media result in concern about crime and drugs as well as in an unwarranted level of fear of crime by citizens (Beckett 1994; Gordon and Heath 1981, 244). In a sense, the media is generating fear among certain populations. Of course, some populations are more fearful than others. The fear of becoming a victim is stronger in metropolitan centers than in the U.S. as a whole (Steel and Steger 1988, 79). "In general, blacks are more fearful than are other racial or ethnic groups, people who are widowed, separated or divorced are more fearful than are the never or currently married, and older people are more fearful than are younger people" (Steel and Steger 1988, 79). Women are more afraid than men, even though men are twice as likely to suffer from crime than women (Steel and Steger 1988, 79).

Because of the media's distortion of crime, the public's concern with crime is a priority. On the whole, the American public considers crime to be an important national problem (Steel and Steger 1988, 79). Public concern about crime issues peaked in the mid 1960s, and crime remains one of the top concerns of Americans today (Marion 1994, 11; Jacob et al. 1982, 6; Cole 1988, 1).

The "shared opinion of a collection of individuals on a common concern" such as crime is called the public opinion about crime (Yeric and Todd 1989). A survey taken in July 1991 by Hart and Teeter (1991) shows that drugs and crime and violence are a top concern among Americans. Their survey results indicate that over one third of respondents feel that drugs are a very serious problem, and that almost one third feel that crime and violence is a very serious problem:

	Drugs	Crime and Violence
Not really a problem	18%	26%
Somewhat a problem	22%	27%
Fairly serious problem	20%	17%
Very serious problem	36%	29%

In general, the public also feels that on the whole crime is increasing. In 1991, researchers asked the public to respond to a question that stated, "In your community, do you think that violent crime is more of a problem than it was 10 years ago, less of a problem than 10 years ago, or is it about the same?" The responses showed the following (Schulman Ronca Bucuvalas, 1991):

37%	About the Same
54%	More
4%	Not Sure
5%	Less

In 1993, a similar question was asked in a survey by Chilton Research Services. This indicated that 86% of people felt that there was more violence in society as a whole than in previous years. 12% felt that there was the same amount, and 2% felt there was less (Chilton Research Services 1993).

When asked if fear of crime has caused people to limit the places they go by themselves, 60% answered yes. 32% of respondents stated that their fear of crime forced them to limit the places or time they went shopping, and 22% have limited the type of places or times they choose to work. Fear of crime forced 25% to install a home security system, and 18% have purchased a weapon (Schulman Ronca Bucuvalas 1991).

A telephone survey of 397 adults showed that the public has strong support for punishment of offenders. However, there was also strong support for rehabilitation, particularly by young, poor, minorities, who are more likely to serve time in prison (McCorkle 1993).

Gallup polls about crime and criminal behavior also indicate the public's concern with crime. For example, a poll taken in September 1990 show that 81% of respondents favor the registration of all handguns, while 17% oppose such a registration. 51% of respondents indicated that there is more crime in their area than there was a year ago, and 18% said less. Finally, 84% of respondents felt that there is more crime in the U.S. than there was a year ago, and only 3% said less (Gallup and Newport 1990). As to the cause of this increase in crime, a 1982 Gallup poll found that nearly two thirds of adults thought that there was a relationship between violence on television and the rising crime rate in the U.S.

The public also has opinions about what to do with those who commit crimes. One survey shows that 54% of respondents favor trying juveniles in adult courts for committing serious property crimes. In addition, more than 70% favored trying juveniles in adult courts for serious violent crimes and for selling large quantities of illegal drugs (Schwartz, Guo and Kerbs 1993).

As to who is better at proposing effective policies, a survey of public opinion shows some mixed feelings. A *Washington Post/ABC News* poll taken in January, 1990, found that 31% of Americans trusted the Democratic party to handle the crime problem, whereas 43% said they trusted the Republican party more. 28% said that the Democrats were better able to reduce the problem of illegal drugs, while 47% said that Republicans were better ("Crime Polls..." 1990, 1557).

Since the media can alter the public's perceptions so readily, it can be utilized by actors in the political system for their advantage. Politicians use the media to build support for their agenda. They can use the media to make appeals to their constituents about current problems and the "best" approach to solve that problem. They also depend upon the media for voter feedback about those same programs.

Why does the media distort the system to such an extent? A primary reason for its inaccurate portrayal of crime stems from the fact that a primary goal of the media is to make money, which is done through sales and advertising (Baker and Meyer 1980). Members of the media are always trying to increase the circulation of their products, which will enable them to charge more for advertising, and ultimately increase their profits.

The media can increase the circulation of its products by publicizing criminal acts. It does this because crime and violence sells. The rate of violence is high in our society, and people are fascinated with it. Therefore, publishing crime stories helps to sell papers or increase a viewing audience. "Within newspapers, crime news accounts for from 4 to 28 percent of all the news reported, averaging about 7 percent overall. Crime news constitutes newspapers' third largest subject category" (Surette 1992, 62). Crime is also an easy subject for reporters to investigate (Gordon and Heath 1981). News stories are available from police (who are viewed as reliable sources of accurate information) twenty-four hours a day, and the basic facts are also made readily available to reporters.

To increase sales, the media must respond to people's desires for stories about crimes rather than technicalities about the cases. The media attempts to make things easy for the public to understand, but then it is forced to omit details. This does not leave the public with a very good understanding of the system and the people who work in it. Overall, "research suggests that media attention to crime has less to do with the crime rate, as such, than with the general news climate, competition among newspapers and television stations" (Scheingold 1984, 55).

It is obvious that the media's impact on criminal justice and public opinion can be enormous. The media, both print and broadcast, has the power to influence people's perceptions about crime and criminal justice. Unfortunately, that power can also be abused by distorting the stages in the system. This leads to a biased public opinion about criminal behavior.

Beyond the power to influence public opinion, the media has many other effects on the system. The second power of the media is its ability to influence the public agenda or shape public policy. The media has the ability to draw attention to an issue, and in essence inform the public about what issues are important and what issues are not. The public, then, demands action from legislators on those particular issues. In short, the media are defining problems that appear on the government's agenda by using (or even forming) the public's concerns, particularly about crime. The media can also keep an issue on the agenda once addressed by an executive or the legislature. If a problem has not been addressed fully, the media can also bring attention to this and demand further action.

In this capacity, the media acts as a "linkage institution" that links the government officials with public opinion. This is important because in theory, the ideas expressed by the public should be reflected in the policies created by the government (Key 1965). "If a representative form of government is assumed, it is likely that the public, at least indirectly, influences the decisions of public officials who depend on their constituents for positions of power" (Riley and Rose 1980). Further, when public opinion changes or shifts, the policies created by the government should reflect those changes (Weissberg 1979; Nice 1983; Page and Shapiro 1983; Erikson 1976; Hartnagel, Creechan and Silverman 1985; Wright, Erikson and McIver 1987; Weber and Shaffer 1972; Johnson and Huff 1987; Hopkins 1974). The ideas expressed by the public in public opinion polls are reflected in the policies created by the government because politicians rely on the public for support of their policies (Light 1984).

To guarantee that legislators are responsive to public opinion, legislators are elected every two, four, or six years. Elections, however, do not ensure that the public's opinions are incorporated into law. One reason is that individual officials can escape responsibility for policies (Van Horn et al. 1992, 8). They can blame inattention or inaction on other politicians. This is often done with criminal justice issues. Republicans will blame Democrats for inaction, and Democrats will blame Republicans for the same thing.

A third power of the media is whistle-blowing (Baker and Meyer 1980). The media oversees the actions of many people, including politicians and actors in the criminal justice field. Reporters investigate these actors to determine if any wrongdoing has taken place, and if so, they publicize it. In essence, this is supposed to keep people honest. A perfect example of the whistle-blowing function of the media is the investigations of the Watergate affair by Woodward and Bernstein (1974). Many argue that the scandal would not have been discovered if it were not for the determination of these reporters in discovering the truth about the activities of the Nixon administration and his Committee to Re-elect the President.

Fourth, the media has the power to cause crime. This can be seen on two levels. First, the media can influence the behavior of individuals when they show very violent acts that are then "copied" by someone who viewed the act. These crimes are termed "copycat" crimes because they are crimes influenced by publicity about an original crime. These offenders incorporate major elements of the original crime into their own.

Also, violence on television is often accused of causing violence in children. Some children are more likely to be violent or aggressive after watching violent television programs. Two federal government reports concerning research on television and crime were published on this problem. In 1972, a report to the surgeon general reported that there was a "tentative indication of a causal relationship" between violent television and violent behavior. The second report, sponsored by the National Institution of Mental Health (NIMH) concluded more strongly that television causes violence (Milavsky; Parenti 1992, 118).

A fifth power of the media is the ability to influence the trial process. The media can cover a story so extensively before it comes to trial so that finding a jury without bias is difficult. Excessive media coverage has affected trials to such an extent that the convictions have been overturned. This is especially true when the case involves a terrible crime or when the defendants are celebrities. The coverage of these trials is rarely neutral, which can make the jurors prejudge a case (Levine 1992). Current examples of extensive media coverage include the cases of William Kennedy Smith, Jeffrey Dahmer and O.J. Simpson. The media coverage of these cases affected the public's opinions about these individuals, which may have prevented a fair and unbiased jury trial.

Sixth, the media has the potential power to deter future or potential criminal behavior. This is a theoretical argument based on deterrence theory, which provides that information about the plight of other criminals will deter potential criminals from committing crimes. In other words, if a person considering committing a criminal act sees another person being punished for that same act (or even a similar act), they may choose to refrain from committing the offensive behavior. The media plays a key role because it has the responsibility of publicizing the punishments for criminal behavior. This publicity may deter others from committing similar acts. This is called general deterrence, and is the process of deterring members of the general public from committing crimes through publicizing criminal punishments.

Seventh, the media can also help to fight crime. Through the public service announcements about issues such as the dangers involved with drug abuse, the media may be helping someone choose not to abuse drugs. Other programs such as McGruff the Crime Dog may also help to alleviate some crime. Crime-Watchers and neighborhood crime watch programs also help to increase awareness about criminal behavior.

Conclusion

The mass media and public opinion both play important roles in the American political process, and both have substantial impact on criminal justice. Both print and broadcast media serve as the principal means by which the public opinion is expressed and altered (Van Horn et al. 1992, 224). "Newspapers, television networks, and local stations shape the news and thus influence public officials and public opinion" (Van Horn et al. 1992, 234). Unfortunately, the ability of the media to influence public concern with crime is based more upon their coverage rather than upon reported crime (Beckett 1994). This means that the public's concern with crime is not based on reality, but rather on the media's perception of reality, which tends to be biased. Because of the biased presentation of crime issues and events, the public's opinion about crime and related policies may also be distorted.

The media can affect crime in other ways as well. For example, the media can influence the government's agenda, it can act as a whistle blower against wrongdoing, it can cause or even prevent crime, and it can affect the jury's opinion about certain publicized cases. Through these powers, the media has become a very powerful political institution that has major impact on the criminal justice system directly and indirectly.

Bibliography

Baker, R., and F.A. Meyer, Jr. 1980. *The Criminal Justice Game*. North Scituate, Mass: Duxbury Press.

Beckett, K. 1994. "Setting the Public Agenda: 'Street Crime' and Drug Use in American Politics." *Social Problems* 41: 435-447.

Chilton Research Services Survey. 1993. April 15-19, cited in *American Enterprise*. 1993. 4: 77-82.

Cole, G.F. 1988. *Criminal Justice: Law and Politics*. Pacific Grove, Calif: Brooks/Cole Publishing Company.

"Crime Polls and Politics." 1990. *Congressional Quarterly Weekly Reports* 48: 1557.

Dye, T., H. Zeigler, and S.R. Lichter. 1992. *American Politics in the Media Age*. Pacific Grove, CA: Brooks/Cole Publishing Co.

Erikson, R.S. 1976. "The Relationship between Public Opinion and State Policy: A New Look Based on Some Forgotten Data." *American Journal of Political Science* 20: 25-36.

Gallup, G., Jr., and F. Newport. 1990. "Support for Gun Control at All-Time High." *The Gallup Poll Monthly*. 300:34-39.

Gordon, M.T. and L. Heath. 1981. "The News Business, Crime and Fear." In D.A. Lewis (Ed.), *Reactions to Crime*. Beverly Hills: Sage Publications.

Hart, P. and R. Teeter. 1991. Survey taken for NBC News and Newsweek July 14-18, 1991. Cited in *American Enterprise*. 4: 77-82.

Hartnagel, T.F., J.J. Creechan, and R.A. Silverman. 1985. "Public Opinion and the Legalization of Abortion." *Canadian Review of Sociology and Anthropology* 22: 411-430.

Hellinger, D. and D.R. Judd. 1994. *The Democratic Facade*. Belmont, CA: Wadsworth Publishing Company.

Hopkins, A.H. 1974. "Opinion Publics and Support for Public Policy in the American States." *American Journal of Political Science* 18:

167-177.

Jacob, H., R. Lineberry, A.M. Heinze, J.A. Beecher, J. Moran, and D.H. Swank. 1982. *Governmental Responses to Crime: Crime on Urrban Agendas*. Washington, D.C.: U.S. Department of Justice, National Institute of Justice.

Johnson, B.A. and R.C. Huff. 1987. "Public Opinion and Criminal Justice Policy Formation." *Criminal Justice Policy Review* 2: 118-132.

Key, V.O. 1965. *Public Opinion and American Democracy*. New York: Alfred A. Knopf.

Levine, J.P. 1992. *Juries and Politics*. Pacific Grove, CA: Brooks/Cole Publishing Company.

Lewis, D. 1981. "Crime in the Media: Introduction." In D.A. Lewis (Ed.), *Reactions to Crime*. Beverly Hills: Sage Publications.

Light, P.C. 1984. "The Presidential Policy Stream." In M. Nelson (Ed.), *The Presidency and the Political System*. Washington, D.C.: CQ Press.

Marion, N.E. 1994. *A History of Federal Crime Control Initaitives, 1960-1993*. Westport, Conn: Praeger Press.

McCorkle, R.C. 1993. "Research Note: Punishment and Rehabilitate? Public Attitudes Toward Six Common Crimes." *Crime and Delinquency* 39: 240-52.

Milavsky, J.R. "TV and Violence." Washington, D.C.: National Institute of Justice.

Newman, G.R. 1990. "Popular Culture and Criminal Justice: A Preliminary Analysis." *Journal of Crime and Justice* 18: 261-274.

Nice, D.C. 1983. "Representation in the States: Policymaking and Ideology." *Social Science Quarterly* 64: 404-411.

Page, B. and R. Shapiro. 1983. "Effects of Public Opinion on Policy." *American Political Science Review* 77: 175-190.

Parenti, M. 1992. *Make-Believe Media: The Politics of Entertainment*. New York: St. Martin's Press.

Parenti, M. 1993. *Inventing Reality: The Politics of News Media*. New York: St. Martin's Press.

Riley, P.J. and V.M. Rose. 1980. "Public vs. Elite Opinion on Correctional Reform: Implications for Social Policy." *Journal of Criminal Justice* 8: 345-356.

Scheingold, S,A. 1984. *The Politics of Law and Order*. New York: Longman Inc.

Schulman Ronca Bucuvalas for the National Victim Center, March 8-17, 1991. Cited in *American Enterprise* 2: 74-82.

Schwartz, I.M., S.Guo, and J,J. Kerbs. 1993. "The Impact of Demographic Variables on Public Opinion Regarding Juvenile Justice:

Implications for Public Policy." *Crime and Delinquency* 39: 5-28.

Steel, B.S. and M.A.E. Steger. 1988. "Crime: Due Process Liberalism Versus Law-and-Order Conservatism." In R. Tatalovich and B.W. Daynes (Eds.), *Social Regulatory Policy*. Boulder: Westview Press.

Surette, R. 1992. *Media, Crime and Criminal Justice*. Pacific Grove, Calif: Brooks/Cole Publishing Company.

Van Horn, C.E., D.C. Baumer, and W.T. Gormley, Jr. 1992. *Politics and Public Policy*. Washington, D.C.: CQ Press.

Weber, R.E. and W.R. Shaffer. 1972. "Public Opinion and American State Policy-Making." *Midwest Journal of Political Science* 4: 683-699.

Weissberg, R. 1976. *Public Opinion and Popular Government*. Englewood Cliffs, NJ: Prentice-Hall, Inc.

Woodward, B. and C. Bernstein. 1974. *All the President's Men*. New York: Simon and Schuster.

Wright, G.C., R.S. Erikson, and J.P. McIver. 1987. "Public Opinion and Policy Liberalism in the American States." *American Journal of Political Science* 31: 980-1001.

Yeric, J.L. and J.R. Todd. 1989. *Public Opinion: The Visible Politics*. Itasca, Illinois: F.E. Peacock Publishers, Inc.

Nine

Conclusion

NO LONGER IS criminal justice focused only upon police, courts and corrections. It has evolved into an interdisciplinary field of study that incorporates ideas from many different fields. The more recent policy-oriented approach to the study of politics and American government has provided criminologists with a new perspective on the study of crime. Criminologists can now use the theories and ideas from political science to gain a better understanding of the criminal justice system and how it changes and evolves as the political forces change and evolve. An analysis of the criminal justice system would be incomplete without an examination of the influence of political institutions.

The relationships between criminal justice and political science are simple and complex at the same time. There are both direct and indirect political influences that have dramatic impact on the justice system. One of the most obvious direct political impacts is the legislative role played by members of Congress. In this role, the Congress defines illegal behavior and potential punishments. But Congress has other, less obvious, impacts as well, including the allocation of money and providing a public forum for debate about current justice issues. Congress also acts as a check on the behavior of the president and the judiciary, and it can react to the behavior of these other political actors. For example, when the president proposes legislation, Congress can choose to act or not. Or when the courts make an unpopular decision, Congress can choose to make legislation that "over-rides" the court decision.

The president also has a direct impact on criminal justice through his agenda-setting function. In this role, the president defines the importance that anti-crime measures will receive in an administration. Some presidents have placed crime at the top of their agendas, whereas others have decided that other issues were more pressing. The president has other, indirect roles as well. These include the nominations of various bureaucrats to serve in agencies, the granting of pardons for past criminal convictions, and a leadership role for his political party. The president, like Congress, can react to the actions of the other two branches of government. He can choose to react to Congress's legislative action by signing a bill or vetoing it, or he can react to a judicial decision by proposing legislation. In addition, the president can influence the policy coming out of the courts by appointing justices with a similar ideological background.

The branch of government that is probably most widely recognized as impacting criminal justice is the judicial branch, or the court system. The courts' power to decide cases and to review previous decisions has enormous impact on the creation of criminal justice policy. This policy is based on a judge's ideological positions, and on the type of judicial position he or she holds. Judicial politics and power are also evident in the recruitment process, especially at the federal level. The courts have the power to review the policies made by both the president and Congress, and the power to declare them constitutional or not.

Beyond the three branches of government as defined in the Constitution, other political institutions are also very active in criminal justice issues. One of these consists in the bureaucracies

that have been set up by Congress to implement policies created
in the legislature. These bureaucracies have great discretion to
define (or to create) policies that are left undefined by Congress.
Many different agencies have been created to deal only with
criminal justice concerns, some of which were described earlier.

Another political institution that has great impact on the
justice system consists in interest groups. These groups have
different techniques to influence the legislative process in such a
way that the final policy reflects their particular interests.
Groups differ as to their size, their leadership, and their effectiveness in influencing the process. Despite these differences, these
groups all attempt to influence Congress by providing information about the problem or even policy proposals. Some groups,
such as the ACLU or ABA, attempt to influence the courts
through legal battles. The groups also have an influence on the
behavior of the president by promising or taking away electoral
support. Some of the groups that have formed around criminal
justice issues were also defined earlier.

Occasionally, the issues that are of concern to interest groups
have also become issues in presidential elections. It has only been
since the 1960s that crime has played a role in these campaigns,
and it has not played a role in every campaign since then.
Nonetheless, these campaigns have helped to raise crime control
from a states' rights issue to a federal issue.

Crime as a campaign issue has also helped to influence the
public's opinion about crime. These opinions are also influenced
by the media, which tends to broadcast distorted information
about the justice system and elements of it. This leads to an
uninformed constituency base that is still demanding action from
legislators.

It is obvious that the relationship between criminal justice
and politics is sometimes simple and sometimes more complex.
The future of this relationship will continue to see the two areas
becoming even more intertwined as crime continues to rise and
crime control remains a top national concern of citizens. People
will continue to look toward the federal government for action
that will help to solve the crime problem in our nation, and
politicians will be forced to place anti-crime initiatives on their
agendas.

Bibliography

Bibliography

Allen, F.A. 1981. *The Decline of the Rehabilitative Ideal*. New Haven, Conn: Yale University Press.

Almond, G.A. and S. Verba. 1970. "Political Participation and Democratic Stability." In E.A. Nordlinger (Ed.), *Politics and Society*. Englewood Cliffs, New Jersey: Prentice Hall-Inc.

Almond, G.A. and S. Verba. 1963. *The Civic Culture: Political Attitudes and Democracy in Five Nations*. Englewood Cliffs, New Jersey: Prentice Hall-Inc.

Anderson, J.E. 1990. *Public Policymaking: An Introduction*. Boston: Houghton Mifflin Company.

Bachrach, P. 1967. *The Theory of Democratic Elitism*. Boston: Little, Brown and Company.

Baker, R., and F.A. Meyer, Jr. 1980. *The Criminal Justice Game*. North Scituate, Mass: Duxbury Press.

Ball, L.D. 1978. *The United States Marshals of New Mexico and Arizona Territories, 1846-1912*. Albuquerque: University of New Mexico Press.

Barber, J.D. 1986. "The Presidency: What Americans Want." In P.S.

Nivola and D.H. Rosenbloom (Eds.), *Classic Readings in American Politics*. New York: St. Martin's Press.

Barker, E. 1980. *Social Contract*. New York: Oxford University Press.

Beard, C.A. 1990. "Framing the Constitution." In P. Woll (Ed.), *American Government: Readings and Cases*. Glenview, Illinois: Scott, Foresman Company.

Beard, C.A. and M.B. Vagts. 1957. *The Economic Basis of Politics and Related Writings by Charles A. Beard*. New York: Vintage Books, Inc.

Beccarria, C. 1963. *On Crimes and Punishment*. H. Paolucci (Ed.). New York: Bobbs-Merrill, Inc.

Beccarria, C. 1979. "On Crimes and Punishment." In J.E. Jacoby (Ed.), *Classics of Criminology*. Prospect Heights, Illinois: Waveland Press, Inc.

Beckett, K. 1994. "Setting the Public Agenda: 'Street Crime' and Drug Use in American Politics." *Social Problems* 41: 425-447.

Berry, J. 1984. *The Interest Group Society*. Boston: Little, Brown and Company.

Birkby, R. 1985. "The Courts: 40 More Years." In M. Nelson (Ed.), *The Elections of 1984*. Washington, D.C.: CQ Press.

Biskupic, J. 1991. "Letter-Writing and Campaigns." *Congressional Quarterly Weekly Report* 49: 183.

Biskupic, J. 1991a. "Bush Boosts Bench Strength of Conservative Judges." *Congressional Quarterly Weekly Report* 49:171-174.

Biskupic, J. 1991b. "1990-91 Term Marked by Surge in Conservative Judges." *Congressional Quarterly Weekly Report* 49:1829-1831.

Biskupic, J. 1991c. "Democrats to Push Thomas on Abortion, Other Views." *Congressional Quarterly Weekly Report* 49:1826-1828.

Biskupic, J. 1991d. "Thomas Hearings Illustrate Politics of the Process." *Congressional Quarterly Weekly Report* 49:2688-2689.

Brewster, L.G. and M.E. Brown. 1994. *The Public Agenda*. New York: St. Martin's Press.

Calder, J.D. 1982. "Presidents and Crime Control: Kennedy, Johnson and Nixon and the Influences of Ideology" *Presidential Studies Quarterly* 12: 574-589.

Chilton Research Services, Survey from April 15-19, 1993. Cited in *American Enterprise* "Public Opinion and Demographic Report: Crime Concerns." 4: 77-82.

Cobb, R.W. and C.D. Elder. 1982. "Issue Creation and Agenda Building." In J.E. Anderson (Ed.), *Cases in Public Policy-Making*. New York: Holt, Rinehart and Winston.

Cole, G.F. 1988a. *Criminal Justice: Law and Politics*. Pacific Grove, CA: Brooks/Cole Publishing Company.

Cole, G.F. 1988b. "The Paradigm Change in Criminal Justice: The Contribution of Political Science." *Journal of Contemporary Criminal Justice* 4: 49-56.

"Complete Text of the 1968 Republican Platform." 1968. *Congressional Quarterly Almanac* 24: 987-994.

"Congress Enacts Five Anti-Crime Bills." 1961. *Congressional Quarterly Almanac* 17: 381-85.

Cook, E.F. 1984. *A Detailed Analysis of the Constitution*. Totowa, New Jersey: Rowman and Allanheld, Publishers.

"Crime." 1972. *Congressional Quarterly Weekly Report* 30: 2221.

"Crime: Again a Presidential Election Year Issue." 1972. *Congressional Quarterly Weekly Report* 30: 2323-2325.

"Crime Polls and Politics." 1990. *Congressional Quarterly Weekly Reports* 48: 1557.

Cronin, T.E. 1990. "The Swelling of the Presidency: Can Anyone Reverse the Tide?" in P. Woll (Ed.), *American Government: Readings and Cases*. Glenview Heights, Illinois: Scott, Foresman and Company.

Cronin, T.E., T.Z. Cronin, and M.E. Milakovich. 1981. *U.S. v. Crime in the Streets*. Bloomington: Indiana University Press.

Dahl, R.A. 1961. *Who Governs?* New Haven: Yale University Press.

Dahl, R.A. 1956. *A Preface to Democratic Theory*. Chicago: University of Chicago Press.

Davidson, R.H. and W.J. Oleszek. 1985. *Congress and Its Members*. Washington, D.C.: CQ Press.

Davis, S. 1993. "Power on the Court: Chief Justice Rehnquist's Opinion Assignments." In R.B. Ripley and E.E. Slotnick (Eds.), *Readings in American Government and Politics*. Belmont, CA: Wadsworth Publishing Company.

Daynes, B.W. 1988. "Pornography: Freedom of Expression or Societal Degradation?" In R. Tatalovich and B.W. Daynes (Eds.), *Social Regulatory Policy*. Boulder: Westview Press.

Deering, C.J. and S.S. Smith. 1985. "Subcommittees in Congress." In L.C. Dodd and B.C. Oppenheimer (Eds.), *Congress Reconsidered*. Washington, D.C.: CQ Press.

Department of the Treasury. 1991. "U.S. Customs Service": Mission and Organization." Washington, D.C.: Department of the Treasury, U.S. Customs Service.

Department of the Treasury. 1992. "BATF Quarterly Report." Washington, D.C.: Department of the Treasury.

Dolbeare, K.M. and L.J. Medcalf. 1993. *American Ideologies Today*. New York: McGraw-Hill.

Dumhoff, W. 1990. *The Power Elite and the State: How Policy is Made in America*. New York: Aldine de Gruyter.

Durkheim, E. 1960. *The Division of Labor in Society*. G. Simpson, (Trans.), Glencoe, Ill: Free Press.

Dye, T.R. 1991. "Elitism in a Democracy." In G. McKenna and S. Feingold (Eds.), *Taking Sides*. Guilford, Conn:Dushkin Publishing Group, Inc.

Dye, T., H. Zeigler, and S.R. Lichter. 1992. *American Politics in the Media Age*. Pacific Grove, Calif: Brooks/Cole Publishing Co.

Eagleton, T.F. 1991. *Issues in Business and Government*. Englewood Cliffs, N.J.: Prentice Hall.

Edelman, M. 1985. *The Symbolic Uses of Politics*. Urbana: University of Illinois Press.

Edwards, G.C. III and S.J. Wayne. 1985. *Presidential Leadership*. New York: St. Martin's Press.

Elder, C.D. and R.W. Cobb. 1983. *Political Use of Symbols*. New York: Longman Press.

Elshtain, J.B. 1989. "Issues and Themes in the 1988 Campaign." In M. Nelson (Ed.), *The Elections of 1988*. Washington, D.C: CQ Press.

Erikson, R.S. 1976. "The Relationship Between Public Opinion and State Policy: A New Look Based on Some Forgotten Data."*American Journal of Political Science* 20: 25-36.

Erikson, R.S. and G.C. Wright. 1985. "Voters, Candidates, and Issues in Congressional Elections." In L.C. Dodd and B.C. Oppenheimer (Eds.), *Congress Reconsidered*. Washington, D.C.: CQ Press.

Eyestone, R. 1978. *From Social Issues to Public Policy*. New York: John Wiley and Sons.

Fairchild, E.S. 1981. "Interest Groups in the Criminal Justice Process." *Journal of Criminal Justice* 9: 181-194.

Fairchild, E. and V.A. Webb. 1985. *The Politics of Crime and Criminal Justice*. Beverly Hills: Sage Publications.

Ferguson, T. and J. Rogers. 1986. *Right Turn: The Decline of the Democrats and the Future of American Politics*. New York: Hill and Wang.

Friedman, W. 1959.*Law in a Changing Society*. Berkeley: University of California Press.

Galliher, J.F. and J.Ray Cross. 1982. "Symbolic Severity in the Land of Easy Virtue: Nevada's High Marihuana Penalty." *Social Problems* 29: 380-386.

Gallup, G. Jr. and F. Newport. 1990. "Support for Gun Control at All-Time High." *The Gallup Poll Monthly* 300: 34-39.

Gawthrop, L.C. 1969. *Bureaucratic Behavior in the Executive Branch*. New York: The Free Press.

Glick, H.R. 1993. *Courts, Politics and Justice*. New York: McGraw Hill,

Inc.

Gordon, G.J. 1992. *Public Administration in America*. New York: St. Martin's Press.

Gordon, M.T. and L. Heath. 1981. "The News Business, Crime and Fear." In D.A. Lewis (Ed.), *Reactions to Crime*. Beverly Hills: Sage Publications.

Gould, L.L. 1993. *1968: The Election that Changed America*. Chicago: Ivan R. Dee.

Greeley, A.M. 1991. "Building Coalitions." In G. McKenna and S. Feingold (Eds.), *Taking Sides*. Guilford, Conn: Dushkin Publishing Group, Inc.

Gulick, L. 1985. "Policy Roles of Public Administrators." In P. Schorr (Ed.), *Critical Cornerstones of Public Administration*. Boston, Mass: Oelgeschlager, Gunn and Hain, Publishers, Inc.

Hallett, M.A. and D.J. Palumbo. 1993. *U.S. Criminal Justice Interest Groups*. Westport, Conn: Greenwood Press.

Hamilton, A., J. Jay, and J. Madison. 1961. *The Federalist Papers*. C. Rossiter (Ed.), New York: New American Library.

Hart, P. and R. Teeter. 1991. Survey for NBC News and Newsweek, July 14-18, 1991. Cited in *American Enterprise* "Public Opinion and Demographic Report: Crime Concerns." 4: 77-82.

Hartnagel, T.F., J. Creechan, and R.A. Silverman. 1985. "Public Opinion and the Legalization of Abortion."*Canadian Review of Sociology and Anthropology* 22: 411-430.

Hellinger, D. and D.R. Judd. 1994. *The Democratic Facade*. Belmont, CA: Wadsworth Publishing Company.

Hobbes, T. 1983.*Leviathan*. C.B. Macpherson (Ed.), New York: Penguin Books.

Hopkins, A.H. 1974. "Opinion Publics and Support for Public Policy in the American States." *American Journal of Political Science* 18: 167-177.

Idelson, H. 1993a. "Downsizing of Drug Czar Office Draws Mixed Reviews." *Congressional Quarterly Weekly Report* 51:320.

Idelson, H. 1993b. "Special Report: Law Enforcement." *Congressional Quarterly Weekly Report* 51:378.

Idelson, H. 1993c. "Reno's Confirmation was Easy: The Hard Work Lies Ahead." *Congressional Quarterly Weekly Report* 51: 601-602.

Idelson, H. 1993d. "Gun Rights and Restrictions: The Territory Reconfigured." *Congressional Quarterly Weekly Report* 51: 1021-1026.

Jacob, H., R. Lineberry, A.M. Heinz, J.A. Beecher, J. Moran, and D.H. Swank, 1982. *Governmental Responses to Crime: Crime on Urban Agendas*. Washington, D.C.: U.S. Department of Justice, National Institute of Justice.

Jacob, H. 1986. *Law and Politics in the United States*. Boston: Little, Brown and Company.

Johnson, B.A. and R.C. Huff. 1997. "Public Opinion and Criminal Justice Policy Formation." *Criminal Justice Policy Review* 2: 118-1132.

Johnson, C.A. and B.C. Canon. 1984. *Judicial Policies: Implementation and Impact*. Washington, D.C.: CQ Press.

"Johnson, GOP Vie for Election-Year Anticrime Program" 1968. *Congressional Quarterly Weekly Report* 26: 392-394.

Kessel, J.H. 1992. *Presidential Campaign Politics*. Pacific Grove, CA: Brooks/Cole Publishing Company.

Key, V.O., Jr. 1965. *Public Opinion and American Democracy*. New York: Alfred A. Knopf.

Key, V.O., Jr. 1990. "Pressure Groups." In Peter Woll (Ed.), *American Government: Readings and Cases*. Glenview, Illinois: Scott, Foresman and Company.

Koenig, L.W. 1985. "Reconsidering the American Presidency and its Relation to Congress and the Bureaucracy." In P. Schorr (Ed.), *Critical Cornerstones of Public Administration*. Boston, Mass: Oelgeschlager, Gunn and Hain, Publishers, Inc.

Lasswell, H. 1936. *Politics: Who Gets What, When, How*. New York: McGraw-Hill.

"Law Enforcement/Judiciary." 1982. *Congressional Quarterly Almanac* 38: 20-21.

"Law Enforcement/Judiciary." 1983. *Congressional Quarterly Weekly Report* 41: 149.

"LEAA Goes Out of Business." 1982. *Congressional Quarterly Almanac* 38: 378-379.

Levine, J.P. 1992. *Juries and Politics*. Pacific Grove, CA: Brooks/Cole Publishing Co.

Lewis, D. 1981. "Crime in the Media: Introduction." In D.A. Lewis (Ed.), *Reactions to Crime*. Beverly Hills: Sage Publications.

Light, P.C. 1984. "The Presidential Policy Stream." In M. Nelson (Ed.), *The Presidency and the Political System*. Washington, D.C.: CQ Press.

Light, P.C. 1983. *The President's Agenda*. Baltimore: The Johns Hopkins University Press.

Locke, J. 1980. *Second Treatise of Government*. C.B. Macpherson (Ed.). Indianapolis: Hackett Publishing Company.

Loftus, T. 1994. *The Art of Legislative Politics*. Washington, D.C.: CQ Press.

Long, N.E. 1978. "Power and Administration." In F.E. Rourke (Ed.), *Bureaucratic Power in National Politics*. Boston: Little, Brown and

Company.

Lowi, T.J. and B. Ginsberg. 1990. *American Government: Freedom and Power*. New York: W.W. Norton and Company.

Marion, N.E. 1994. *A History of Federal Crime Control Initiatives, 1960-1993*. Westport, CT: Praeger Publishers.

Martin, J.M. 1994. *Lessons from the Hill: The Legislative Journey of an Education Program*. New York: St. Martin's Press.

Masci, D. 1994a. "The Modified Crime Bill." *Congressional Quarterly Weekly Report* 52: 2490.

Masci, D. 1994b. "$30 Billion Anti-Crime Bill Heads to Clinton's Desk." *Congressional Quarterly Weekly Report* 52: 2488-2493.

McCorkle, R.C. 1993. "Research Note: Punishment and Rehabilitate? Public Attitudes Toward Six Common Crimes." *Crime and Delinquency* 39: 240-52.

McKenna, G., and S. Feingold (Eds.), 1991. *Taking Sides*. Guilford, Conn.: Dushkin Publishing Group, Inc.

Mead, W.B. 1987. *The United States Constitution: Personalities, Principles and Issues*. Columbia: S.C.: University of South Carolina Press.

Melone, A.P. and R. Slagter. 1983. "Interest Group Politics and the Reform of the Federal Criminal Code." In S. Nagel, E. Fairchild and A. Champagne (Eds.), *The Political Science of Criminal Justice*. Springfield, Illinois: Charles C. Thomas, Publisher.

Merton, R.K. 1970. "Bureaucratic Structure and Bureaucratic Behavior." In E.A. Nordlinger (Ed.), *Politics and Society*. Englewood Cliffs, New Jersey: Prentice-Hall, Inc.

Milavsky, J.R. "TV and Violence." Washington, D.C.: National Institute of Justice.

Mill, J.S. 1984. *On Liberty*. Gertrude Himmelfarb (Ed.). New York: Penguin Books.

Mill, J.S. 1983. *Three Essays*. Richard Wollheim (Ed.). New York: Oxford University Press.

Miller, W.B. 1973. "Ideology and Criminal Justice Policy: Some Current Issues." *Journal of Criminal Law and Criminology* 64: 141-162.

Mills, C.W. 1956. *The Power Elite*. New York: Oxford University Press.

Misner, G.E. 1981. *Criminal Justice Studies: Their Transdisciplinary Nature*. St. Louis: C.V. Mosby Company.

Murphy, W. 1964. *Elements of Judicial Strategy*. Chicago: University of Chicago Press.

Nagel, S., E. Fairchild, and A. Champagne (Eds.). 1983. *The Political Science of Criminal Justice*. Springfield, Illinois: Charles C. Thomas, Publisher.

Nelson, M. 1984. "Evaluating the Presidency." In M. Nelson (Ed.), *The*

Presidency and the Political System. Washington, D.C.: CQ Press.

Newman, G.R. 1990. "Popular Culture and Criminal Justice: A Preliminary Analysis." *Journal of Criminal Justice* 18: 261-74.

Nice, D.C. 1983. "Representation in the States: Policymaking and Ideology." *Social Science Quarterly* 64: 404-411.

"Nixon." 1968. *Congressional Quarterly Weekly Report* 26: 88.

O'Brien, D.M. 1993.*Storm Center*. New York: W.W. Norton and Company.

Page, B.I. and R.Y. Shapiro. 1993. "Presidents as Opinion Leaders." In R.B. Ripley and E.E. Slotnick (Eds.),*Readings in American Government and Politics*. Belmont, CA: Wadsworth Publishing Company.

Page, B. and R. Shapiro. 1983. "Effects of Public Opinion on Policy." *American Political Science Review* 77: 175-190.

Parenti, M. 1992. *Make-Believe Media: The Politics of Entertainment*. New York: St. Martin's Press.

Parenti, M. 1993. *Inventing Reality: The Politics of News Media*. New York: St. Martin's Press.

"Passage of Major Crime Bills Not Likely in 1965." 1965. *Congressional Quarterly Weekly Report* 23: 1881-1884.

Polsby, N.W. and A. Wildavsky. 1980.*Presidential Elections*. New York: Free Press.

Pomper, G. 1989.*The Election of 1988*. Chatham, N.J.: Chatham House Publishers, Inc.

Popkin, J. 1994. "A Case of Too Much Candor." *U.S. News and World Report* 117: 31.

Price, D.E. 1985. "Congressional Committees in the Policy Process." In L.C. Dodd and B.C. Oppenheimer (Eds.), *Congress Reconsidered*. Washington, D.C.: CQ Press.

Prince, C.E. and M. Keller. 1989. *The U.S. Customs Service*. Washington, D.C.: Department of the Treasury, U.S. Customs Service.

Quinney, R. 1969. *Crime and Justice in Society*. Boston: Little, Brown and Company.

"Reagan Makes Crime a Campaign Issue." 1984*Congressional Quarterly Weekly Report* 42: 2451.

Redman, E. 1973. *The Dance of Legislation*. New York: Simon and Schuster.

"Remarks Made in Omaha, Nebraska." 1970. *Public Papers of the President*. 1011-1019.

Reich, R.B. 1994. "Policy Making in a Democracy." In F.S. Lane (Ed.), *Current Issues in Public Administration*. New York: St. Martin's Press.

"Responsibility for Rising Crime Rates an Election Issue." 1964. *Congressional Quarterly Weekly Report* 22: 2602-2605.

Riley, P.J. and V.M. Rose. 1980. "Public vs. Elite Opinion on Correctional Reform: Implications for Social Policy." *Journal of Criminal Justice* 8: 345-356.

Ripley, R. 1983. *Congress: Process and Policy*. New York: W.W. Norton and Company.

Rosch, J. 1985. "Crime as an Issue in American Politics." In E. Fairchild and V.A. Webb (Eds.), *The Politics of Crime and Criminal Justice*. Beverly Hills: Sage Publications.

Rosenthal, A. 1988. "Foes Accuse Bush Campaign of Inflaming Racial Tension." *New York Times* October 24, 1988, p. A1.

Rossiter, C. 1990. "The Presidency: Focus on Leadership." In P. Woll (Ed.), *American Government: Readings and Cases*. Glenview, Illinois: Scott, Foresman and Company.

Rourke, F.E. 1984. "The Presidency and the Bureaucracy: Strategic Alternatives." In M. Nelson (Ed.), *The Presidency and the Political System*. Washington, D.C.: CQ Press.

Rourke, F.E. 1978. *Bureaucratic Power in National Politics*. Boston: Little, Brown and Company.

Rousseau, J.J. 1983. *On the Social Contract*. D. Cress (Ed.). Indianapolis: Hackett Publishing Company.

Rousseau, J.J. 1964. *The First and Second Discourses*. R.D. Masters (Ed.). New York: St. Martin's Press.

Salmore, S.A. and B.G. Salmore. 1985. *Candidates, Parties and Campaigns*. Washington, D.C.: CQ Press.

Scammon, R. and B. Wattenberg. 1970. *The Real Majority*. New York: Coward-McCann.

Scheingold, S.A. 1984. *The Politics of Law and Order*. New York: Longman Inc.

Schlozman, K.L. and J.T. Tierney. 1993. "More of the Same: Washington Pressure Group Activity in a Decade of Change." In R.B. Ripley and E.E. Slotnick (Eds.), *Readings in American Government and Politics*. Belmont, CA: Wadsworth Publishing Company.

Schulman Ronca Bucuvalas for the National Victim Center, March 8-17, 1991. Cited in "Crime, Cops and Courts" *American Enterprise* 2: 74-82.

Schwartz, I.M., S. Guo, and J.J. Kerbs. 1993. "The Impact of Demographic Variables on Public Opinion Regarding Juvenile Justice: Implications for Public Policy." *Crime and Delinquency* 39: 5-28.

Scigliano, R. 1984. "The Presidency and the Judiciary." In M. Nelson (Ed.), *The Presidency and the Political System*. Washington, D.C.: CQ Press.

"Select Committee Labor Investigations." 1959. *Congressional Quarterly Almanac* 15: 731-741.

"Select Labor Committee Labor Issues Final Report." 1960. *Congressional Quarterly Almanac* 16: 699-705.

Senna, J.J. and L.J. Siegel. 1990. *Introduction to Criminal Justice*. St. Paul: West Publishing.

Shafer, B.E. 1989. "'Exceptionalism' in American Politics" *P.S.: Political Science and Politics* 22: 588-594.

Simon, H.A., D.W. Smithburg and V.A. Thompson. 1978. "The Struggle for Organizational Control." In F.E. Rourke (Ed.), *Bureaucratic Power in National Politics*. Boston: Little, Brown and Company.

Smith, C.E. 1992. *Politics in Constitutional Law: Cases and Questions*. Chicago: Nelson-Hall Publishers.

Smith, H. 1988. *The Power Game*. New York: Ballantine Books.

Sommer, R.L. 1993. *The History of the U.S. Marshals*. Philadelphia: Courage Books.

Spitzer, R.J. 1988. "Gun Control: Constitutional Mandate or Myth?" in R. Tatalovich and B.W. Daynes (Eds.), *Social Regulatory Policy*. Boulder: Westview Press.

Steel, B.S. and M.A.E. Steger. 1988. "Crime: Due Process Liberalism Versus Law-and-Order Conservatism." In R. Tatalovich and B.W. Daynes (Eds.), *Social Regulatory Policy*. Boulder: Westview Press.

Stenson, K. and D. Cowell. 1991. *The Politics of Crime Control*. London: Sage Publications.

Stolz, B.A. 1983. "Congress and Capital Punishment." *Law and Policy Quarterly* 5: 157-180.

Stolz, B.A. 1992. "Congress and the War on Drugs: An Exercise in Symbolic Politics." *Journal of Crime and Justice* 15: 119-135.

Surette, R. 1992. *Media, Crime and Criminal Justice*. Pacific Grove, Calif: Brooks/Cole Publishing Company.

Truman, D.B. 1951. *The Governmental Process*. New York: Knopf.

U.S. Customs Service. 1989. "International Accomplishments, 1982-1989." Washington, D.C.: U.S. Customs Service.

U.S. Customs Service. 1984. "The International Activities of the U.S. Customs Service." Washington, D.C.: U.S. Customs Service.

Van Horn, C.E., D.C. Baumer, and W.T. Gormley, Jr. 1992. *Politics and Public Policy*. Washington, D.C.: CQ Press.

Walker, S. 1994. *Sense and Nonsense about Crime and Drugs*. Belmont, California: Wadsworth Publishing Co.

Walker, S. 1990. *In Defense of American Liberties*. New York: Oxford University Press.

Weber, R.E. and W.R. Shaffer. 1972. "Public Opinion and American State Policy-Making." *Midwest Journal of Political Science* 4: 683-699.

Weissberg, R. 1976. *Public Opinion and Popular Government*. Englewood Cliffs, N.J.: Prentice-Hall, Inc.

Wilson, J.Q. 1978. "The Rise of the Bureaucratic State." In F.E. Rourke (Ed.),*Bureaucratic Power in National Politics*. Boston: Little, Brown and Company.

Wilson, J.Q. 1975. *Thinking About Crime*. New York: Vintage Books.

Wise, C.R. 1991. *The Dynamics of Legislation*. San Francisco: Jossey-Bass Publishers.

Wittenberg, E. and E. Wittenberg. 1990. *How to Win in Washington*. Cambridge, MA: Basil Blackwell, Inc.

Wong, B. 1993. "Anti-Crime Bill Chronology." *Congressional Quarterly Weekly Report* 53: 2979.

Woodward, B. and C. Bernstein. 1974. *All the President's Men*. New York: Simon and Schuster.

Wright, G.C., R.S. Erikson, and J.P. McIver. 1987. "Public Opinion and Policy Liberalism in the American States." *American Journal of Political Science* 31: 980-1001.

Yeric, J.L. and J.R. Todd. 1989. *Public Opinion: The Visible Politics*. Itasca, Illinois: F.E. Peacock Publishers, Inc.

Zuckman, J. 1993. "The President's Call to Serve is Clear but Undefined." *Congressional Quarterly Weekly Report* 53: 218-221.

Index

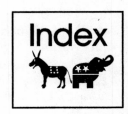

A Current Affair, 107
agendas, 29-30
  institutional (governmental
    agendas), 29-30
  President Bush's, 42
  President Carter's, 40
  President Clinton's, 43
  President Ford's, 39
  President Johnson's, 34
  President Kennedy's, 33
  President Nixon's, 37-8
  President Reagan's, 41
  systemic agendas, 29
American Bar Association (ABA),
  79, 80, 85, 120
American Civil Liberties Union
(ACLU), 79, 80, 102, 120
American Journal, 107
American Liberty League, 80
America's Most Wanted, 107
An Organization of Americans
  for Legal Reform (HALT),
  84-5
anti-crime bills, 1, 2, 41, 43, 44
Abscam Scandal, 10
Attorney General's Office, 68

Beccaria, Cesare, 2
Bork, Robert, 56

Boschwitz, Rudy, 78
Brady Bill, 19-20, 21, 24, 30, 44,
  103
Brady Handgun Violence Protection Act (see Brady Bill)
Brennan, William, 57
Brown v. Board of Education
(1954), 54
Bureau of Alcohol, Firearms and
  Tobacco, 43, 73
Bureau of Justice Assistance, 71
Bureau of Justice Statistics, 71
Bureau of Prisons, 69-70
bureaucracies, 2, 15, 18, 38, 62-
  75, 119-20
  criminal justice bureaucracies,
    68-73
  powers of, 63-5
  sources of power, 65-7
  weaknesses of, 67
Bush, George, 8, 42-3, 45, 50, 51,
  57, 101-3

campaigns and elections, 8, 10,
  93-105, 120
campaign issues, 94-5
  personal, 94-5
  positional, 94-5
  substantive 94-5

symbolic, 94-5
valence, 94-5
Carter, James "Jimmy", 31, 40-1,
  45, 99-100
Central Intelligence Agency
  (CIA), 15, 30
Citizen's Committee for the
  Right to Keep and Bear Arms,
  82
Clinton, Bill, 8, 43-5, 102-3
Coalition to Stop Gun Violence,
  83
commissions, 36-7
  Commission on Obscenity and
    Pornography, 36
  National Commission on
    Reform of the Federal Crimi-
    nal Laws, 37
  National Commission to
    Abolish the Federal Death
    Penalty, 37
  President's Commission on
    Law Enforcement and Admin-
    istration of Justice, 36
  Study on Needs in Corrections,
    36
  Study on the Judiciary, 37
conference committees, 17-8, 20
Conflict Theory, 21-2
congress and crime, 4, 14-27, 119
  legislative process, 17-9
  powers, 14-6, 24-5
Consensus Theory, 21
conservatives, 9
Cops, 107
courts, 2, 4, 18, 39, 40, 48-61, 119
  and interest groups, 80
  Burger, 50-1, 59
  decisions of, 53-4
  overcrowding of, 39-40
  politics and, 54-5
  powers of, 48
  recruitment of Justices, 55-8

relations with Presidents and
  Congress, 58-9
  Warren, 50, 51, 59

death penalty, 41, 43, 44
Department of Corrections, 15
Department of Justice, 15, 30,
  38, 68
District of Columbia, 36, 37, 41
Dole, Robert, Senator, 20
drug abuse, 7, 35, 37-8, 39, 40,
  41, 42, 102, 103
drug czar, 43, 101
Drug Enforcement Administra-
  tion (DEA), 38
Drug Policy Foundation, 89
Dukakis, Kitty, 8, 101
Dukakis, Michael, 8, 101-2
Dumhoff, William, 23

Eisenhower, Dwight D., 31
elections (see Campaigns and
  elections)
elitism, 23, 77
exclusionary rule, 41, 43

Federal Bar Association, 86-7
Federal Bureau of Investigation
  (FBI), 15, 30, 31, 43, 70, 98-9,
  108
Federal Criminal Code, 39, 40
Federal Firearms Act, 35
Federalist 10, 22, 76
Federalist 78, 55
Ford, Gerald, 31, 39-40, 45, 50,
  99-100
48 Hours, 107
Fraternal Order of Police (FOP),
  88

Gantt, Harvey B., 78
Ginsburg, Douglas H., 56
Goldwater, Barry, 8, 95-6, 97

gun control, 15, 21, 30, 35-6, 39,
    40, 41-2, 44, 81-3, see also
    Brady Bill

habeas corpus, 33, 41, 43, 44
Handgun Control Inc., 78, 82
Harkin, Tom, 78
Harris v. New York (1971), 51
Helms, Jesse, 78
Hill, Anita, 57
Hobbes, Thomas, 4-5
Hoffa, James, 31
Horton, Willie, 8, 101-2
House Crime Subcommittee, 19
House Judiciary Committee, 19
House Rules Committee, 19
Humphrey, Hubert, 97-8
hyperpluralsim, 23, 77

insanity defense, 43
interest groups, 2, 22-3, 76-92,
    120
    and Courts, 80
    criminal justice interest
        groups, 80-90
Iran-Contra Affair, 10

Johnson, Lyndon, 8, 34-7, 38, 40,
    41, 45, 56, 59, 95-6, 97-8
juvenile crime, 33-4, 36, 40, 44

Kennedy, Anthony, 56
Kennedy, John, 33-4, 45, 59, 98
Kennedy, Robert, 7, 33, 34, 45,
    96
Kennedy, Ted, 57
King, Martin Luther, 96

Lasswell, Herbert, 3
Law Enforcement Assistance
    Administration (LEAA), 3, 15,
    39, 41
Legal Services Corporation

(LSC), 38
legislative process, 16
Levin, Carl, 78
liberals, 9
Lincoln, Abraham, 10
Locke, John, 4

Madison, James, 22, 76
mandatory sentences, 39, 40, 42,
    44
Manion, Daniel, 58
Marbury v. Madison (1964), 54
Marshall, Thurgood, 56, 57
McClellan, John L., Senator, 7
McGovern, George, 98-9
media, 2, 106-117
Mill, John Stuart, 5
Mills, C. Wright, 23
Miranda v. Arizona (1966), 51
Mitchell, John, 98
Mondale, Walter, 100-1
Mountain States Legal Founda-
    tion, 80

National Association of Attor-
    neys General, 85-6
National Association of Chiefs of
    Police, 88
National Association of Crime
    Victim Compensation Boards,
    84
National Association of Criminal
    Justice Planners, 90
National Center for Prosecution
    of Child Abuse, 84
National Center on Institutions
    and Alternatives, 87-8
National Committee Against
    Repressive Legislation, 89-90
National Institute of Justice, 71
National Organization for the
    Reform of Marijuana Laws
    (NORML), 88-9

National Organization for Victim
Assistance, 83
National Organization for
Women (NOW), 81
National Rifleman's Association
(NRA), 19, 78, 81-2, 103
Nixon, Richard, 31, 37-8, 39, 40,
41, 45, 50, 59, 96-9, 100
Noriega, Manuel, 102

Office of Justice Programs, 71
Office of Juvenile Justice and
Delinquency Programs, 71-2
Office of National Drug Control
Policy, 43
Office for Victims of Crime, 72
organized crime, 7, 33, 35, 37, 40

pardons, presidential, 31
pluralism, 22, 77
political culture, 22
pornography, 42
power, 4,5
concurrent powers, 6
enumerated powers, 5
exclusive powers, 6
implied powers, 6
in Conflict theory, 22
of bureaucracies, 63-5
of Congress, 14-6, 24-5
of Courts, 48, 52-3
of media, 107-14
of Presidents, 28-32, 45
presidents, 28-47
and crime control policies, 32-
45, 119
and powers, 28-32, 45
veto power, 18, 31
Prime Time Live, 107
public opinion, 2, 30, 106-17, 120

Reagan, Ronald, 8, 10, 19, 30, 31,
41-2, 45, 50, 51, 100-1

reported crime, 8
Roe v. Wade (1973), 54
Rousseau, Jean-Jacques, 4

Schuette, Bill, 78
Senate Select Committee on
Improper Activities, 7, 33
Sentencing Project, 87
Shaw, Bernard, 101
Simon, Paul, 78
Smith, Peter, 78
Social Contract, 4, 14
Solicitor General, 69
Souter, David, 57
Special Action Office of Drug
Abuse Prevention, 38
State Justice Institute, 44
State of Nature, 4
Symbolic Policies, 23-2

Tauke, Tom, 78
Texas v. Johnson (1989), 58
Thomas, Clarence, 56-7

Uniform Crime Reports, 8, 70
United States v. Eichman (1990),
58
Unsoeld, Jolene, 78
U.S. Customs Service, 72-3
U.S. Marshal's Service, 15, 32,
43, 70
U.S. Parole Board, 15

victims of crime, 39, 42, 83, 84

Wallace, George, 98
Watergate, 10, 31, 32
Weber, Max, 63
Wellstone, Paul, 78